R E A D Y - T O - U S E
Fine Motor Skills & Handwriting Activities
for
Young Children

Joanne M. Landy
& Keith R. Burridge

THE CENTER FOR APPLIED RESEARCH IN EDUCATION
West Nyack, NY 10994

COMPLETE MO**S PROGRAM**

Library of Congress Cataloging-in-Publication Data

Landy, Joanne M.
    Ready-to-use fine motor skills & handwriting activities for
 young children / Joanne M. Landy, Keith R. Burridge ;   illustrations
 by Joanne M. Landy.
        p.   cm. — (Complete Motor Skills Activities Program)
    Includes bibliographical references
    ISBN 0–13–013942–4
    1. Movement education.   2. Motor learning.   3. Penmanship—Study
 and teaching (Elementary)   I. Burridge, Keith R.   II. Title.
 III. Series: Landy, Joanne M.   Complete Motor Skills Activities
 Program.
 GV452.L353   1999
 372.86'8—dc21   99–30193
                                                             CIP

Acquisitions Editor: *Susan Kolwicz*
Production Editor: *Mariann Hutlak*
Interior Design/Formatter: *Dee Coroneos*

© 1999 *by* Joanne M. Landy and Keith R. Burridge

Printed in the United States of America

10 9 8 7 6 5 4

ISBN 0-13-013942-4

ATTENTION: CORPORATIONS AND SCHOOLS

The Center for Applied Research in Education books are available at quantity discounts with bulk purchase for educational, business, or sales promotional use. For information, please write to: Prentice Hall Direct, Special Sales, 240 Frisch Court, Paramus, NJ 07652. Please supply: title of book, ISBN, quantity, how the book will be used, date needed.

**THE CENTER FOR APPLIED RESEARCH
IN EDUCATION**
West Nyack, NY 10994

On the World Wide Web at http://www.phdirect.com

DEDICATION

In memory of Joanne's husband,
Professor Max Landy, and his
dedication to the teaching profession.

ABOUT THE AUTHORS

Joanne M. Landy earned a B.Ed. degree, graduating with Great Distinction from the University of Regina, Saskatchewan, Canada in 1974. She also completed a post graduate international P.E. study course through Concordia University in Montreal, Quebec, and a Personal Trainer course through Renouf Fitness Academy in Perth.

Joanne's professional background includes 10 years of secondary teaching in physical education/health and mathematics; 10 years of specialist teaching in primary physical education, as well as several years of University demonstration teaching in P.E. methodology and pedagogy programs, in the Canadian school system. In 1988 Joanne and her late husband, Professor Maxwell Landy, were part of the leadership team at the National Youth Foundation Fitness Camp in Los Angeles. She is also co-author with Maxwell of the four-book series *Complete Physical Education Activities Program* (Parker Publishing, 1993).

Joanne now resides with her children in Perth and operates a Lifestyle Education consulting business which provides in–depth workshops and inservicing in physical education at all levels, including University P.E. teacher training programs. She is also a member of the Board of Consultants for Sportsmart/Sportime Australia (Melbourne-based), which markets a wide range of innovative and educational manipulative equipment in physical education. In the recreational areas, Joanne has been instrumental in developing and coordinating youth activity-based programs which include a Junior Basketball Skills Development Program, a "Tune-Up-Kids" program for young children from 5–12 years of age which focuses on development of fundamental movement skills, and a personal development program for teenage girls (13–18 years of age) called "On the Move." She has also set up "Tune Up" programs for adults and runs team-building and motivational sessions for school staffs, corporate business groups, and other community groups.

Joanne has presented at major HPERD (Health, Physical Education, Recreation and Dance) conferences in North America, Australia, and New Zealand. She also has facilitated many workshops in primary/secondary P.E. teaching at the University of Western Australia, Notre Dame College of Education, Western Washington University, Washington State, University of Regina, Saskatchewan, and major university centers throughout New Zealand. This year, Joanne lectured at Murdoch University, Education Faculty, in the Primary Physical Education teacher training program. She maintains an active lifestyle and is still involved in many sports on a regular basis.

Keith R. Burridge earned a Dip. Ed. from Nedlands Secondary Teachers College, followed by a B.P.E. degree (1978) and M.Ed. from the University of Western Australia, Perth. Keith's professional background includes 15 years as a secondary physical education and science teacher, 5 years as a primary physical education specialist, and 4 years of special education working with children with movement difficulties. From

1995–97 he was employed by the Department of Education of Western Australia (Perth) as a school Development Officer in Physical Education and was responsible for professional development in P.E. for over 80 schools. He has represented Australia at the elite level in canoeing.

Keith was one of the key writers for the Western Australia Department of Education's 1998 Fundamental Movement Skills Package. He has lectured at Notre Dame College of Education and Murdoch University, and facilitated programs for early childhood education. Keith has presented F.M.S. and best practices in teaching workshops throughout Western Australia. He is the co-author with Joanne Landy of the newly released book *50 Simple Things You Can Do to Raise a Child Who is Physically Fit* (Macmillan, 1997). As a F.M.S. specialist, Keith has contributed in the writing of a book called *Why Bright Children Fail* (Hammond, 1996). He is also the designer for a K-3 computer assessment package for identifying children at an early age who have coordination problems. This program is in operation in over 400 schools in Western Australia.

Presently, Keith is teaching at Willeton Senior High School in Perth and piloting a special program to work with children at educational risk.

ACKNOWLEDGMENT

We would like to thank our publisher and editor, Win Huppuch and Susan Kolwicz, and the production staff Diane Turso, Dee Coroneos, and Mariann Hutlak at Prentice Hall for their enthusiastic support and editorial and production expertise in the making of this book.

INTRODUCTION TO COMPLETE MOTOR SKILLS ACTIVITIES PROGRAM

The *Complete Motor Skills Activities Program* consists of three books:

➤ Ready-to-Use Fundamental Motor Skills & Movement Activities for Young Children

➤ Ready-to-Use Fine Motor Skills & Handwriting Activities for Young Children

➤ Ready-to-Use Motor Skills & Movement Station Lesson Plans for Young Children

This program has been designed as a motor skills program for teachers, professionals, and parents in related fields (remedial, rehabilitation, and medical areas), working in the school environment, the home environment, or the community environment to assist children who have coordination difficulties in the performance and mastering of fundamental movement skills.

The focus of this program is to provide enjoyable developmentally-appropriate movement experiences in the teaching of these fundamental movement skills so that the children gain both competence and confidence in successfully performing these skills.

We emphasize that if the strategies are to be successful, teachers and parents need to be aware that although children may be able to perform the tasks adequately in terms of task completion, focus must be directed to *how* the task is completed; that is, focus must be directed toward quality of the movement—not just the outcome of the movement.

FINE MOTOR SKILLS & HANDWRITING

This book has been produced to provide educators, parents and other professionals working with children, an overview of the key elements of fine motor control and handwriting. It was never meant to be a resource for extracting reproducible material, but a guide to developmental aspects of these areas and examples of practical activities that will be useful in determining when and what should be included in teaching and remediation programs.

MANIPULATIVE ACTIVITIES

Most manipulative activities require the use of the two hands working together to perform the task These are referred to as **bi-manual activities.** Single handed manipulative activities are referred to as **uni-manual activities,** for example, opening a door. The third type of manipulative activities are **graphic activities** which include drawing and handwriting.

In general, children show the most improvement in simple fine motor control behaviors from 4 to 6 years, whereas more complex control behaviors tend to improve gradually from 5 to 12 years. Isolated finger, hand, wrist and foot movements tend to improve significantly from 5 to 8 years.

Word processing has created an alternative method of graphic communication to handwriting, however in schools and especially in the early years, handwriting still remains the main method by which children communicate their thoughts and ideas. Historically, teachers have been encouraged to teach handwriting models and children have adapted as best they can to the model. Realistically, we should be attempting to adapt the model to fit the child's needs and physical abilities.

The *method* of teaching handwriting is, therefore, far more important than the model itself and teaching handwriting should reflect this. The old saying "you can please all of the people some of the time and some of the people all of the time" is no truer than when teaching children handwriting. Handwriting is as individual as the child. All the elements of a particular model are not going to suit all children. Variations exist in adult handwriting; why not with children's handwriting? After all, a letter is just a visible trace of a hand movement and we all move in different ways, especially in the quality of our movements.

Motor memory is also an important component to this learning process and relates to the child's ability to visually and auditorially copy single movements, movement patterns, and rhythm patterns.

Current research suggests that if children do not reach a degree of competence and confidence in fundamental movement skills by the sixth grade, they will not engage in regular physical activity or sports for the rest of their lives.

SEVEN ESSENTIAL KEYS

Successful skills teaching in fundamental movement skills can result if you incorporate the following seven essential keys:

1. *Show enthusiasm, care, and interest.* These are qualities that cannot be written into any program. They come from *you,* and without them the program is not going to be so effective as it could be.

2. *Use visual demonstration with instruction* whenever possible. You may even need to physically move the child through some of the actions.

3. *Give praise, encouragement, and feedback.* These are an essential part of the learning process. Simply to say "do your best" does not bring about a constructive change. What is needed is good information about techniques and feedback (information about what the child has done). For example, "I watched the way you held the ball correctly in your fingers" or "That was a great effort; this time let's put your other foot forward."

4. *Create a positive, fun learning environment.* Sometimes we get preoccupied with telling the child what he or she is doing wrong or what he or she has not done instead of focusing on what he or she should be doing. A positive comment indicates to a child approval; the child can then develop trust and a willingness to keep trying.

5. ***Keep the information simple and easy to follow.*** Teaching by small-step progression is ideal. Progress may be a lot slower than you think and so patience definitely becomes a virtue.

6. ***Keep the home play sessions shorter, more frequent, yet allowing for ample practice.*** Some parents may be too enthusiastic and make the session simply too long. By keeping the sessions shorter, you can ensure that physical and mental fatigue do not become a factor and that the child's interest level is sustained.

7. ***Avoid showing frustration; be patient.*** If *you* feel frustrated, imagine how the child must feel. Frustration on your part is easily picked up by the child and compounds difficulties. Try saying "I think this is a good place to stop for today. Let's continue tomorrow."

ABOUT THIS BOOK

This book covers four important areas: An Insight Into Fine-Motor Skills, Preparatory and Manipulative Activities, Development of Pencil and Paper Activities, and Handwriting Development. It contains many practical activities that will be useful in determining when and what should be included in teaching and remediation programs for children who display difficulties with selected fine-motor skills or may have difficulties in many areas, including handwriting. If a child does not experience difficulties in these areas, this book is still valuable since it promotes correct skills and provides valuable play and learning time.

➤ *An Insight into Fine-Motor Skills:* This section consists of important facts for teachers and parents, such as fine-motor checklists, observable behaviors of children with fine-motor difficulties, and ideas for programming. It is imperative that adults have an understanding and knowledge of the importance of fine-motor development on which to base teaching and remediation strategies.

➤ *Preparatory and Manipulative Activities:* Included in this section are spatial, memory, and body image and body management activities which provide children with the movement vocabulary and awareness important for further development. This section also contains information and activity examples for development of uni-manual and bi-manual manipulative activities, which together form the foundations of any fine-motor program.

➤ *Development of Pencil and Paper Skills:* This section consists of a developmental approach to these skills, emphasizing the need to provide children with clear goals and teaching instruction when they are completing these tasks. This section provides educators and parents with examples of the *type* of activities that can be used for development in these areas.

➤ *Handwriting Development:* This section is a developmental look at handwriting and the components that should be taught. Apart from information on writing aspects, this section contains tips that will assist children who are experiencing difficulties. Also included are a number of checklists, which provide a useful means of monitoring development in the different areas of handwriting. At the end of this section are reproducible masters for fading techniques, which provide an excellent resource for remediation of handwriting difficulties.

Knowing that children need to be given the best possible start to life and learning, we recommend this book as a valuable resource to achieve this goal. Children move to learn, but first of all, they most learn to move!

Joanne M. Landy & Keith R. Burridge

CONTENTS

SECTION 1
BODY MANAGEMENT

SECTION 2
FINGER ACTIVITIES

SECTION 3
MANIPULATION ACTIVITIES

SECTION 4
PENCIL-AND-PAPER ACTIVITIES

SECTION 5
HANDWRITING

SECTION 6
HANDWRITING ACTIVITIES

FINE-MOTOR SKILLS

Fine-motor coordination involves the ability to control the small muscles of the body and is usually defined as the ability to coordinate the action of the eyes and hands together in performing precise manipulative movements (eye–hand coordination). The early forerunners of fine-motor control appear to be the reflex grasp and avoidance reactions that become integrated and refined with increasing age and experience.

Most manipulative activities require the use of the two hands working together to perform the task. These are referred to as *bi-manual activities.* Single-handed manipulative tasks are referred to as *uni-manual activities;* for example, opening a door. The third type of manipulative activities are *graphic activities* which include drawing and handwriting.

In general, children show the most improvement in simple fine-motor control behaviors from 4 to 6 years, whereas more complex control behaviors tend to improve gradually from 5 to 12 years. Isolated finger, hand, wrist, and foot movements tend to improve significantly from 5 to 8 years.

Vision is known to play an important role in fine-motor control. Continued visual experience is necessary for feedback and refinement of early guided-hand responses.

Kinesthetic input from receptors in the muscles, joints, tendons, and skin also provide essential information for development and refinement of fine-motor actions.

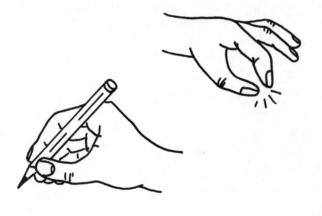

WHY TEACH FINE-MOTOR?

Children explore the environment by moving and interacting with it. By manipulating objects and gathering valuable information about the physical characteristics, this eventually provides perceptual information necessary to make future judgments without the need for physical contact. Through a matching of perceptual and motor information, a child can interpret the characteristics of the environment more efficiently.

Young children at school spend approximately 60%–70% of their time completing fine-motor work or activities. Approximately 12% of children experience difficulties in this area.

Proficiency in fine-motor control allows the child to develop skills that will have consequences immediately and in later life.

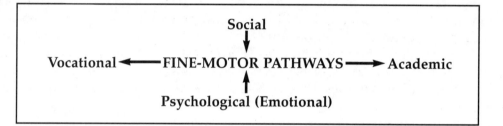

> *Social Consequences.* You cannot hide the way you move. Simple tasks such as tying laces or handling any utensils or objects can cause frustration and embarrassment. The child who has poor coordination begins to wonder why something that is natural and taken for granted is so difficult to perform.

> *Vocational Consequences.* Because a number of vocations—including dentistry, secretarial work, cabinet making, and many others—have a large fine-motor component, the choices for the individual with fine-motor difficulties begin to diminish.

> *Academic Consequences.* Quick and precise handling of concrete objects in mathematics and science becomes difficult. Precision and speed in handwriting and drawing tasks are minimized, affecting the amount of work being completed. When actions are not automatic, the available working memory and attentional space in the brain is taken up with concentrating on the movement rather than the concept being learned and practiced.

➤ *Psychological (Emotional) Consequences.* Children with poor coordination often have unsuccessful experiences in physical activities. As a consequence they can develop frustration, a fear of failure, and rejection which in turn can lead to the development of a negative self-concept and avoidance behaviors. This can dramatically affect classroom performance not only in the fine-motor area but in other areas as well. Research tells us that a child's attitude toward learning in a particular area is at least as important as a child's ability in that area.

THE BEST FORM OF EARLY INTERVENTION IS PREVENTION!

GOALS AND PROGRAMMING FOR A FINE-MOTOR PROGRAM

GOALS

➤ Develop and refine lifestyle manipulative skills.

➤ Develop and refine manipulative skills that will be used throughout a child's educational career.

➤ Promote speed, fluency, and efficiency of movement.

➤ Promote correct temporal and spatial accuracy in movement.

➤ Promote tactile kinesthetic awareness.

➤ Promote and provide a catalyst for transfer of perceptual skills using manipulative activities.

➤ Immerse the child in language.

➤ Provide a stimulating and alternative form of learning.

➤ Establish writing readiness skills.

➤ Provide a developmental program that contains individualized activities that will ensure the child experiences success.

➤ Provide extra time for those children experiencing difficulties.

➤ Promote a nonthreatening environment.

PROGRAM SUGGESTIONS

Traditionally fine-motor activities are presented in an informal way to young children in the education system. As stated previously, a significant percentage of children experience fine-motor difficulties and, as such, this informal presentation and practice of activities is not sufficient for their development in this area. Teachers and parents working with children experiencing difficulties must appreciate that these children need to spend more time practicing if they are to improve.

The following section presents a sequence for teaching children fine-motor and manipulative skills, and provides samples of the types of activities and skills they are trying to achieve in these activities. Although this book has been produced primarily for children experiencing movement learning difficulties in the fine-motor and manipulation areas, the activities can be easily adapted to formal class teaching in early childhood education.

Ideas for uni-manual and bi-manual activities are all around us. All it takes is a little imagination to apply them in a formal setting. The pencil-and-paper activities suggested in this book can be found commercially in many books, but we feel that the requirements of most activities can be produced simply, cheaply, and quickly by teachers and parents. So take the ideas and strategies presented in the following sections, work consistently and patiently with the children, and enjoy and share their progress.

GETTING STARTED

By observing children in informal situations and/or through formal testing procedures, teachers, remedial specialists, and parents can determine where a child is experiencing difficulties, whether it be in all areas of fine-motor control, a specific area, or in a specific skill such as tying laces. With this information, it is then possible to plan appropriate strategies. Some observable behaviors and difficulties that children display, are listed on pages xxv–xxvi.

Below are some suggestions for organizational strategies a teacher, remedial specialist, or parent could employ in a fine-motor program. At this point, it is essential to stress again that providing children the opportunity to practice skills is not enough. Teachers, remedial specialists, and parents should become familiar with the techniques required for successful movement and ensure that the children are being given the appropriate instruction and feedback to achieve quality in these movements. Failure to do this allows the child to practice and develop poor movement habits that are difficult to rectify.

PREREQUISITE SKILLS

Development in the areas of attention, motor memory, body image, spatial awareness, and associated language concepts are important prerequisite abilities. The *Complete Motor Skills Activities Program* provides activities to promote these skills if they have not yet developed adequately.

Young children need to practice visual-motor skills and develop kinesthetic and tactile awareness. They also need to develop abilities such as correct muscle tone, relaxation, rhythm, force control, timing, and estimation skills. These are initially practiced through using manipulative equipment such as scarves, lummi sticks, balloons, and similar types of equipment. As these skills are developing, gradually the demands for greater precision are introduced. A teacher, remedial specialist, or parent can have a child practice these activities in isolation, introduce them as warm-ups (e.g., lummi stick or relaxation activities) before a writing activity or include them in station play as discussed in this book.

Finger activities are also very useful as warm-up activities before commencing other fine-motor activities. If children display specific difficulties with finger isolation, then the exercises themselves can become an individual session.

The following aspects should be covered in a fine-motor program:

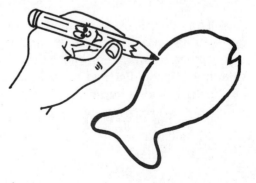

➤ Kinesthetic and tactile awareness

➤ Uni-manual manipulation

➤ Graphic skills

➤ Bi-manual manipulation

In a fine-motor program we can expand on these four areas to include any combinations of the following activities:

1. *Pencil and paper activities.* Drawing, painting, coloring, channeling, tracing, copying, writing, tearing, cutting and folding.

2. *Uni-manual and bi-manual manipulative activities and circuits.*

3. *Commercial games and activities.* These can also be included in the manipulative tasks when doing fine-motor circuits.

4. *Model making,* using different techniques and different materials.

5. *Structured free play.*

6. *Visual motor, kinesthetic, tactile, relaxation exercises, and strengthening activities.*

TIPS:

➤ Use finger exercises. Lummi sticks and manipulo boards are simple and effective activities that can be used daily for short periods to enhance dexterity.

➤ Teach the children what aspects of movement to concentrate on before allowing practice; for example, precision grip. Try to provide feedback as often as possible.

➤ Music creates an excellent working environment.

➤ Teachers have the opportunity to create formal whole-class fine-motor lessons, or to incorporate movement enrichment programs for small groups of children needing assistance. Parents or older students assisting as tutors is an excellent strategy for maximizing teaching and individualizing.

➤ The activities can be made more challenging by introducing time and quantity challenges; i.e., how many or how long. This must only be done when the children are successfully completing the tasks correctly. The activities can also have cognitive concepts added to them as described in Section 3 information on fine-motor boards and activities.

➤ Preparing workbooks is initially time consuming but worth the time and effort when children and tutors know exactly what they are going to do and can record their results.

OBSERVABLE BEHAVIORS OF CHILDREN WITH FINE-MOTOR DIFFICULTIES

OBSERVABLE BEHAVIORS

➤ Difficulty with writing; poor grasp leading to poor form, fluency, and frequent discomfort when writing.

➤ Difficulty controlling speed of movements leading to excessive speed and resultant untidy work, or work not being completed due to overly slow movements.

➤ Difficulty with precision grip and inaccurate release and therefore problems with games that involve placement of pieces; for example, dominoes.

➤ Difficulty with spatial relations leading to difficulties with design and copying.

➤ Tearing paper and/or breaking pencils due to force-control difficulties.

➤ Difficulty with learning to dress and undress.

➤ Preference for outdoor activities.

➤ Clumsiness and frustration: spills food; drops objects; breaks objects.

➤ Frustration towards and/or resistant behavior to manipulative and graphic tasks.

➤ Excessive muscular tension when performing fine-motor tasks.

MANIPULATIVE AND GRAPHIC DIFFICULTIES

➤ *Tremors* or small movements of the hand, which are especially apparent when writing or performing precise manipulative tasks such as threading.

➤ *Poor kinesthetic and tactile awareness* prevents accurate feedback and refining of movements which allow a child to eventually perform a task without looking at their hands; for example, typing/keystroking.

➤ *Hypotonia* or poor muscle tone will affect a child's reaction time and the force applied to tasks such as writing.

➤ *Hypertonia* or excessive muscle tone frequently leads to graphic problems, and/or temporal and spatial judgment difficulties.

➤ *Dyspraxia* or difficulties with motor planning results in poor sequencing of the necessary limb movements to produce a smooth skillful action. Dyspraxic children have difficulties with assembly tasks, self-care skills, and often—through frustration—display excessive tension.

➤ *Manual graphic difficulties* include dysgraphia (writing and/or drawing difficulties) and difficulties with tasks involving dexterity.

➤ *Visual/perceptual-motor difficulties* affect printing and writing skills, and copying and interpreting abilities such as tracking, depth perception, and visual discrimination.

➤ *Synkinesis* is demonstration of uncontrolled and unwanted movements in parts of the body other than that being used for the manipulative task.

STRATEGIES FOR CLASS TEACHING

STRATEGY 1

Children working in groups of four or five are situated around the class and each group has a *particular task* to perform at that station. At the end of 3–5 minutes, the children rotate to another station. The advantage of this is that the tutor has time to reinforce and provide feedback to the children on that particular task, or, if there is a common mistake, explain this to the whole group. Activities can be chosen from the areas of finger exercises and visual-motor skills.

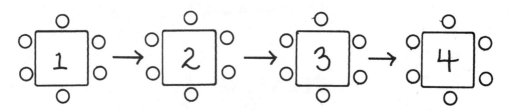

STRATEGY 2

The extension of Strategy 1 is to divide the children into even-numbered groups. At each station have two activities **A + B,** each dealing with a similar concept; for example, a bi-manual task. At each station, the two activities have to be duplicated depending on how many children are in each group. Half of the group completes the station **A** activity (2–3 minutes), while the other half completes the station **B** activity. The groups then rotate activities at that station and, after completing the second task, rotate to the next station. The advantage of this is that the children do not have to stay on the activity for so long. For young children—especially those with attention difficulties—this can be an advantage. As in Strategy 1, the children have a particular task to complete.

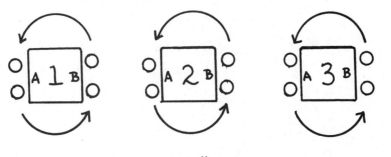

STRATEGY 3

This strategy requires dividing the children into 4–5 groups, with each group working at a station for the entire session. Each station provides a different area of fine-motor control. Because of the number of activities, this strategy is more productive, so we recommend that parents or older students be used as tutors at the stations. For example, group 1 works on pencil-and-paper activities; group 2, model-making; group 3, fine-motor manipulation circuits; group 4, commercial activities and games; and group 5, structured free-play activity. The only group that rotates is group (3) on the circuits (see diagram). At the next session, the groups will remain the same and work at a different station. Therefore, allow 2–4 weeks to complete the rotation depending on how many sessions per week occur.

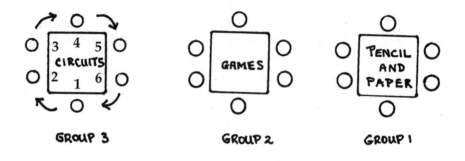

STRATEGY 4

Place the children into groups so that the children will spend 3–5 minutes at each activity. One or two stations are teacher-directed and the other activities involve structured free play. Children become responsible for setting up the activities. (If parent assistance is available, use two teacher-directed stations.)

STRATEGIES FOR A MOVEMENT ENRICHMENT GROUP OR INDIVIDUAL CHILD

Activities of finger exercises and visual motor skills provide excellent warm-up or closing activities.

1. *Concept approach.* All activities are different but concentrate on one concept; for example, bi-manual manipulation. The children rotate around the activities spending 3–5 minutes on each. This strategy is best employed with groups of children who have similar difficulties.

2. *Tabloid approach.* Different activities from the different areas of fine-motor control are presented to the children. This means the children will be able to practice some activities at which they may be already efficient, as well as activities with which they may experience difficulties.

3. *Structured free play.* This provides opportunity for children to have time to experiment with different materials using different methods of manipulation. Feedback on technique is still required.

FINE-MOTOR CHECKLIST

The observation or focus points are provided below in a convenient checklist box, and then followed by a more detailed description of each focus point. We emphasize the importance of being in the know of what skill(s) are involved in the activity the children are performing and being able to observe for correct technique, as well as note areas of difficulty. For example, if the child is cutting out a shape, what skills does he or she need to perform and complete the task? What difficulties does he or she have? How do we correct these difficulties?

Muscle strength
Posture
Muscle tension
Finger isolation
Precision grip
Grip release
Hand size and shape/grip
Hand–eye coordination
Fluency of arm transport
Force control
Manipulation speed
Hand steadiness
Kinesthetic sensitivity

➤ *Muscle strength.* Adequate strength in the postural and manipulative muscles.

➤ *Posture.* Correct posture provides the foundation for correct movements.

➤ *Muscle tension.* Correct muscle tension in muscles (not too loose or too tight).

➤ *Finger isolation.* Refers to the ability of the child to select and accurately move the finger(s) used for a particular task.

➤ *Precision grip.* Grip used to pick up and manipulate objects. Involves the thumb and forefinger and often support from the middle finger.

xxx

➤ *Grip release.* Poor grip release (too quick and forceful).

➤ *Hand size and shape/grip.* Correct hand shape and grip for a particular task; perception, estimation, and control of grip size.

➤ *Hand-eye coordination.* Hand–eye coordination is appropriate (accurate hand/finger placement).

➤ *Fluency of arm transport.* Action of the shoulders, arm, wrist, and fingers is fluent and the action of the body movements is in the correct order.

➤ *Force control.* Controlling the amount of force required for manipulation.

➤ *Manipulation speed.* Control of the speed of movement (not too fast or too slow).

➤ *Hand steadiness.* Hand movements are steady (reduction of tremors).

➤ *Kinesthetic sensitivity.* The feedback from muscles, joints, skin, and tendons that is used to assist in refining movements.

ASSESSING STUDENTS

When looking at assessment in movement—whether it be gross motor or fine motor—a number of stages need to be considered dependent upon what level of understanding you require of student performance. Below is a guideline as to some aspects of assessment that need to be considered.

STAGE 1: GLOBAL ASSESSMENT

During this first stage, you should observe and monitor the children in formal and informal situations. You should make qualitative judgments on the children's level of coordination. For those children appearing to have difficulties, you should make some anecdotal comments.

This monitoring is ongoing and provides the foundation for reporting.

STAGE 2: SCREENING

This optional stage involves assessing children on the standardized tests that are available and recognized as reliable and valid.

The results provide important information on the levels of coordination of the children in these areas. This information is extremely useful for class and individual student programming.

STAGE 3: ONGOING QUALITATIVE ASSESSMENT

This stage involves your monitoring and making qualitative observations in the different skill areas. Using checklists, information can be gained that provides the foundations for teaching, individual correction, and feedback in the class. Again, the need is for you to be familiar with the key movement points given for individual skills.

STAGE 4: INDIVIDUAL ASSESSMENT FOR THE PURPOSE OF REMEDIATION

If, from your global observations and from standardized testing, a child is recorded as experiencing difficulties, then you should use checklists to try and find the most probable cause of the difficulty. Do not eliminate the possibility that the cause of the difficulty is sensory in nature and that referral to a medical professional might be required.

IMPORTANT FACTS FOR PARENTS

➤ Parents should have reasonable expectations for their child's abilities and for potential skill changes.

➤ Children with movement difficulties often do not learn so well or so quickly using conventional methods of instruction, as do coordinated children.

➤ Parents need to be aware that children experiencing movement difficulties require more time to learn a skill. They need constant feedback and quite often need to be physically taken through movements (kinesthetic assistance).

➤ Parents should be aware that some difficulties will disappear with maturity; some will not. The longer we allow inefficient physical movement to continue, such as incorrect handwriting grip, the harder it becomes to correct because the child practices poor movements which become habits, and then these have to be undone. Also, if these difficulties are left too long, some children begin to display avoidance behavior because they are not experiencing success.

➤ Identifying the physical problems early can result in a favorable prognosis for improvement. However, this requires consistent, cooperative, and effective intervention by the school and by parents.

➤ Try to make your child as independent as possible. To do this you must resist the temptation to complete the tasks for him or her, including such daily requirements as tying shoelaces, cutting food, and dressing. Instead, be there to assist your child to complete the task.

➤ If your child does have a specific weakness in one or two areas, we recommend that you try to spend three 15-minute sessions per week, focusing on these areas of weakness in addition to the normal home play.

➤ It is very important to promote the strengths of the children as well as assisting with their difficulties. You can achieve this by choosing some of the activities that you know your child is good at; for example, the child may have difficulties tying his shoelaces, but is great at cutting out shapes; therefore, do some cutting sessions or include cutting as an enrichment session.

Be patient with your child because it does take longer for children to learn skills than we think. Praise the child's efforts as well—we all need encouragement. Try to be consistent in following this program.

SECTION 1

BODY MANAGEMENT

MOTOR MEMORY

Motor memory relates to your child's ability to visually and auditorially copy movements, movement patterns, and rhythm patterns. If your child experiences difficulties in this area, have a doctor check your child's eyesight and hearing.

Start with one movement and then increase the number (one movement for each age year). The first stage is to have the child remember the moves in any order and then in the correct sequence.

1. Copying hand movements; for example: fist, palm up, palm down, hand sideways

2. Copying touching movements to different body parts

3. Copying body movements (whole body, limb and finger movements)

4. Copying clapping rhythms; foot-stomping; finger-snapping

5. Copying grid patterns; grid patterns can also be completed on paper

6. Movement sequencing; for example: walking on all fours, rolling, hopping

2.   3.

Ask child to follow directions after you have completed your instructions.

1. Move 1 space to the left.

2. Move 2 spaces forward (up on paper).

3. Move 3 spaces to the right.

4. Move 1 space backward (down on the paper).

SPATIAL AWARENESS

Children need to understand spatial language both verbally and physically before they can successfully move around the graphic environment. Below are the more common terms they need to know: near/far; beside/away; under/over; up/down; in/out; on/off; square; side-on; diagonal; in front of/behind/next to; left/right; forward/backward/sideways; inside/outside; fast/slow; high/low; along/between; front/middle/back; top/bottom; around/through; start/finish; join/apart; first/second; next to/space.

Shape language: circle, square, triangle, rectangle, etc.

Size language: big/bigger; small/smaller; little/large

Time language: slow/slower; fast/faster

SPATIAL ACTIVITIES

1. Have child sit at a desk in front of a piece of paper with lines drawn from top to bottom and left to right on the paper. Give instructions for child to place stamp stickers on different parts of the paper: at the top; in the middle; on the line going across the page; under the line going across the page; to the right of the line going from top to bottom; between the line going across the page and the bottom of the page.

2. Now have child make continuous pencil tracings to music. When the music stops, child can move the pencil tip (following the spatial instruction) to objects that have been glued or drawn on the paper. Be aware that paper is 2-dimensional so that when using directional language, this has to be related to how the child is looking at the page.

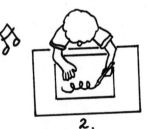

3. Using objects in a room, have child move to music. When the music stops, ask child to move in relation to an object or piece of equipment or another person by saying: stand behind something; sit in front of the chair; kneel beside the table.

SPATIAL ACTIVITIES *(Continued)*

4. In pairs, have one partner do one thing while the other partner does the opposite; e.g., one in front of something while the other is behind; one on something while the other is off; one moves over something while the other moves under, and so on.

4.

5. Use beanbags or folded socks and have child place or throw the object according to certain spatial commands; e.g., put beanbag on top of head; place it behind head; put it on the side of you; in front of you; throw beanbag high into the air.

5.

6. Have child move in spaces to your directions without touching others, furniture, or objects; e.g., move between objects; move around; move under; move over; move on and off; move through; move across, and so on.

7. ***The Dressing/Undressing Game.*** For each child, select a variety of clothes such as socks, shoes with laces, button-up shirt, old tie, jumper, sweater, or jacket. Have child place an item of clothing at each of 5 markers that are spaced 5 meters (15 feet) apart. On signal "Dress!," child goes to a marker, one at a time, and puts on the clothes until fully dressed, then returns to the start. Who can do this the quickest? Who can dress themselves the best? Now reverse this, having child remove clothing and place an item at each marker, then return home.

6.

7.

BODY AND SPATIAL LANGUAGE GAMES

1. ***Body and Number Letters.*** Get into groups of 3 children. Together create different letters or numbers. For example, together make the letter "s," the number "6." Get into groups of 4. Together try to make a two-letter word! How about a double number?

A   T   1.
(Lying on floor)

2. ***Busy Body Parts.*** (Ideally played with 4 or more children.) Call out a body part. Touch this body part to your partner's; e.g., touch your left leg to your partner's left leg. Touch your left shoulder to your partner's right shoulder. Call out another body part. Find a new partner and touch this body part. Continue in this way.

2.

Busy Body Parts

3. ***Simon Says.*** When child hears "Simon says . . ." child responds by doing the task; however, when you ask child to do a task without first saying "Simon says. . ." child does not change from previous task. For example: "Simon says . . . Clap your hands." "Touch your knees!" (Child continues to clap hands.) Add more directional tasks: "Simon says . . . Open and close your left hand." "Simon says, Blink your right eye."

3.

"TOUCH YOUR KNEES"

" CLAP YOUR HANDS"

BODY IMAGE

Children need to have a good understanding of their own body. They should know and be able to name their body parts, where they are in relation to each other, and know which is their right and left side (or sidedness), even though they might not be able to name them. The next step is getting children to respond to the directional language of right and left so that they can combine their knowledge of their body with spatial concepts. Then children will know and can respond to the movement language associated with body image.

Here are some activities you can do together with the children to reinforce this learning.

BODY IMAGE ACTIVITIES

1. On a large piece of paper, have child trace an outline of a friend's body in back-lying position. Together fill in the details of head, ears, eyes, nose, mouth, neck, arms, hands, fingers, belly button, knees, feet, toes.

2. Now have child point to his or her own body parts as you call them out; first with eyes open, then with eyes closed.

2. Touch "ear"

3. "Taste with"

3. Ask child questions such as: "What body part do you blink with? Smell with? Hear with? Taste with? Touch with? Jump with? Sit on? Write with?"

4. Ask child to move just a certain body part at a time; e.g., turn your head from one side to the other; make a fist, then open; bend your knees; wiggle your tongue; snap your fingers; blink one eye then the other, and so on.

"Snap Fingers"

4.

"Blink one eye"

BODY IMAGE ACTIVITIES *(Continued)*

5. Now include specific directionality instructions (right and left) with body movements: shake your left hand; bend your right leg; tap your right fingers on the table; balance on your left leg.

6. Combine with spatial concepts: stand facing the wall; stand side-on with your right side closer to the wall; stand with your back to the chair; sit beside a ball with your left side closer to ball; kneel in front of the table; stand one behind the other.

7. Child now has eyes closed or blindfolded. Name various sounds: ball bouncing; hand clapping; feet stamping; fingers snapping; bell ringing; whistle blowing; drum beating.

8. Identify the direction of the sound. Child hears the sound and must point to the direction.

5. "Balance on left leg"

6. "Face Wall"

"Ball bouncing!"

7.

8.

EXAMPLES OF MOVEMENT LANGUAGE

Circle	Close	Right	Wiggle	Stretch (extend)
Slide	Open	Fast	Shake	Bend (flex)
Tap	Relax	Slow	Clap	Small
Cross	Tighten	Hard	Stamp	Large
Lift	Left	Soft	Snap	

BODY MANAGEMENT—
POSTURE

The importance of promoting good posture at an early age, and having a child do postural exercises correctly and on a regular basis, cannot be emphasized enough. Young children who develop poor posture habits often carry these habits into adulthood with resulting neck and back problems, and learning and movement problems. Children need to "practice" good posture and do flexibility exercises—ideally, every day!

POSTURE ACTIVITIES

Find a "home space" (cannot touch anyone else or anything).

1. *Standing Tall.* Stand tall in your home, feet as wide apart as your shoulders, knees slightly bent. Keep head up and eyes looking straight ahead. Shoulders are back, the back is straight, with hands by your sides. Now give me your best S-M-I-L-E!

2. *Sitting Tall.* Sit tall with head up, eyes looking straight ahead, legs comfortably crossed, and arms resting on knees, fingers interlocked.

3. *Hook Sit.* Take weight on heels of feet, knees bent, and hands supporting weight behind seat.

4. *Walking Tall.* Walk in general space, head up, eyes looking ahead, arms swinging gently out and back, touching heel–toe. Try to walk while balancing a beanbag on your head.

5. *Stopping and Landing.* *Jump Stop:* On signal "Iceberg!" do a little jump, bend your knees, and land on two feet. Hold hands outward for balance.

POSTURE ACTIVITIES *(Continued)*

6. ***Chair Sit.*** Show me how you can sit tall in your chair. Keep your back straight, head up, and feet together or gently crossed at the ankles. Rest your hands on your thighs (upper legs). Breathe normally.

7. ***Hook-Lying.*** Lie on your back with knees bent and feet comfortable and flat on the floor. Press your back against the floor. Check that your back is flat against the floor by seeing if you can slip your hands between back and floor. Breathe normally.

8. ***Front-Lying.*** Lie on your front with legs outstretched and arms relaxed by your sides. Breathe normally.

9. ***Back-Lying.*** Lie on your back with your arms stretched overhead and your legs stretched out behind you.

BODY MANAGEMENT— MUSCLE-TONING

A child needs a stable body to perform fine-motor coordination tasks. For a child to sit "balanced" and perform precise movements—such as handwriting and manipulation tasks—the child must have sufficient strength of trunk and hip areas, as well as muscle strength of fingers, hands, arms, shoulders, neck, and eyes. If the muscles on one side of a joint become stronger than the muscles on the opposite side of that joint, then that body part will be pulled in the direction of the stronger muscles. The following exercises are designed to help strengthen these areas so that the child can perform fine-motor activities better, quicker, and more accurately.

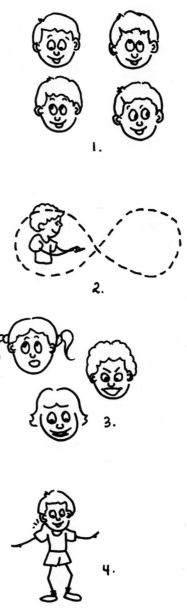

1. *Eye Stare.* Sit tall in your space. Keeping your head straight, let your eyes stare into an imaginary rectangle in front of you. Now move your eyes as I ask you: top right corner; bottom left corner; bottom middle; top left corner; top middle; bottom right corner.

2. *Eye Figure-8's.* Interlock fingers with your pointer fingers straight and together. Trace a large figure-8 with your pointers starting in the center. Let your eyes track the figure-8. Repeat in opposite direction.

3. *Faces.* How many different faces can you make? Now give me your biggest and best smile! Show me how you can make the following sounds and hold for 5 seconds: "Oooh! Aaah! Eeeh!"

4. *Shoulder Shrugs.* Shrug both shoulders at the same time; alternate each shoulder. Shrug and roll your shoulders gently backward; now do alternating shoulder shrugs and rolls.

5. *Angel Wings.* Hold arms out to sides even with your shoulders. Press gently back to squeeze shoulder blades together. Bend at elbows and squeeze again. Continue this pattern.

5.

6. *Finger Push-Ups.* Stand facing a wall, lean forward, and place your palms flat against wall. Push away from the wall with your fingers. Repeat 5–10 times.

6.

7. *Pole Exercises.* Use PVC piping or a broom handle for this exercise, designed to help prevent and correct round shoulders.

   a. In Stand Tall position, grasp pole at ends of stretch pole overhead. Make sure you don't poke your head forward; keep neck straight and chin tucked.

7.a.

   b. Bring pole down behind shoulder blades, keeping your back straight and hold for 5-second count.

b.

   c. Position pole diagonally across your back (as shown). One hand grasps the top of the pole; other hand the bottom, with palms of both hands facing outward. Gently push forward with this bottom hand. Hold for 5 seconds, then reverse.

c.

8. *Knee-to-Chest Exercise.* (To stretch lower back, seat muscles, and hamstrings.) In back-lying position, knees bent, gently draw one knee toward chest using hands on back of thigh. Then straighten leg and point toes towards ceiling. Draw knee back again to the chest, return it to starting position, then repeat with other leg.

8.

9. ***Lower Back Stretcher.*** In back-lying position, draw one knee up to chest and pull thigh down firmly with hands. Return slowly to starting position. Repeat with other knee.

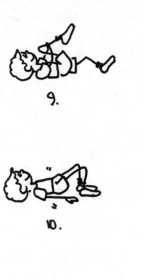

9.

10. ***Bridges.*** (To strengthen hip and seat muscles; to help prevent and correct forward pelvic tilt and lordosis.) In back-lying position, knees bent and feet close to buttocks, tighten your seat muscles, and lift buttocks and lower back off floor. Do not arch the lower back. Hold for 5 seconds; relax. Repeat.

10.

11. ***Arm Lifts.*** (To strengthen shoulder blade muscles and help prevent or correct round shoulders.) Lie on front with arms out to sides and bent at right angles (as shown). Keeping arms in this position and tightening shoulder blade muscles, lift arms as high as possible without raising your head and trunk. Hold; relax.

11.

12. ***Trunk Twister.*** (To increase flexibility of spine.) Lie on your back with arms out at shoulder level and right foot resting on left knee. Twist your lower body by bringing the right knee to touch the floor on the left. Then turn your head to the right. Try to keep your arms and shoulder touching the floor.

12.

13. ***Curl-Up Crunchers.*** (To strengthen the upper abdominals.) In hook-lying position, with palms of hands just lightly covering your ears, curl up until your shoulder blades are off the floor; then curl back down to starting position. Repeat. Don't hold your breath. Breathe out to curl up; breathe in to curl down.

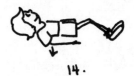

13.

14. ***Pelvic Tilts.*** (To strengthen abdominals and lower back.) In hook-lying position, tighten your tummy muscles and tilt your pelvis backward; that is, try to flatten your lower back against the floor. Hold, then relax. Do NOT hold your breath.

14.

BODY MIMING AND RELAXATION

Body miming and relaxation activities help develop control of our bodies, instill calmness, and help gain concentration and attention skills needed to perform and complete fine-motor tasks. Here are some activities your child can do:

BODY MIMES

Show me how you can be:

➤ narrow, like an arrow

➤ round like a ball

➤ wide and flat like a wall

➤ straight like a pencil

➤ twisted like a corkscrew

➤ curved, like a bow

➤ ice cream melting in the sun

➤ a raggedy-doll flopping around

➤ a tree swaying in the gentle breeze

➤ different letters with your body such as: I, L, J, T, C, Y

➤ with a partner to make a letter shape together; create 2-letter words together: IT, NO (For young children you can show them a letter on a card.)

RELAXATION ACTIVITIES

Lie comfortably on your back on a mat or blanket and close your eyes. Listen to the soothing background music and think of something very pleasant. Relax, breathe easy. When I name a body part, tighten it as much as you can, then relax. For example: squeeze your eyes tight, then open wide. Make a fist with both hands (right/left hands). Push your shoulders to the floor. Squeeze your seat muscles. Tighten your legs, right/left leg. Point your toes. Give me a big smile. Now go "floppy" all over. Try to lift different body parts, checking if that body part is relaxed.

Breathing: Sit quietly with your eyes closed. Listen to your own breathing. Breathe in deeply . . . now breathe out s–l–o–w–l–y.

SECTION 2

FINGER ACTIVITIES

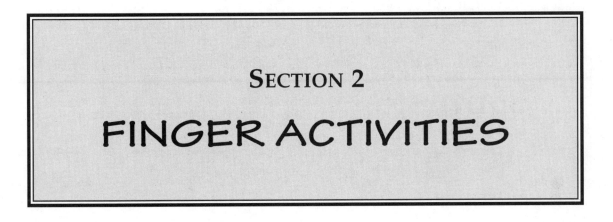

FINGER AEROBICS

The following pages demonstrate some of the many finger exercises that can be used to enhance hand and finger control. We have called them finger aerobics because they are great done to music once the children understand the basics of each exercise. Use these exercises as a warm-up to your writing lesson, fine-motor session, or simply as a break during the day.

FOCUS

Finger dexterity
Sequencing
Fine movement control
Isolation of finger movement

SET-UP

Have child place thumb on the tip of each finger of the same hand. (Before child attempts task, demonstrate first.) Exercises should be carried out with:

➤ preferred hand

➤ non-preferred hand

➤ both hands together

FINGER AEROBICS ACTIVITIES

1. Do aerobic finger movements:

   ➤ slowly, with control (about 1–2 seconds per finger)

   ➤ quickly with control; each finger must be touched separately

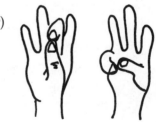

2. Do aerobic finger movements with differing amounts of intensity: some with a light touch to a firm touch.

3. Carry out exercises with:

   ➤ Rhythm using music

   ➤ Eyes closed

   ➤ Fingers numbered 1–5 on each hand; teacher/ parent calls or writes sequence of numbers such as 1–1, 2–2, 3–3, 4–4, 5–5; 5–5, 4–4, 3–3, 2–2, 1–1; 1–1, 3–3, 5–5, 3–3, 1–1; 2–2, 4–4, 5–5, 1–1, etc.

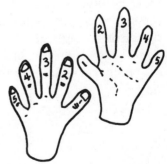

Ensure that fingers separate after each contact.

TRAVELING FINGERS

FOCUS

Finger isolation
Finger identification
Sequencing

SET-UP

Distribute shapes or get children to trace different shapes onto paper and place in front of them.

TRAVELING FINGER ACTIVITIES

1. Child follows teacher's instructions to place required hand (or numbered fingers or fist) on a shape with:

   ➤ preferred hand

   ➤ non-preferred hand

   ➤ both hands

2. Child starts with hands under the table. Using the preferred hand:

   ➤ Single finger to be placed on shape, such as index finger on square

   ➤ Clenched fist on required shape

   ➤ Combination of fingers on shape, such as thumb and little finger, or index finger and ring finger

3. Repeat above with non-preferred hand.

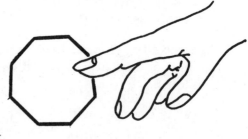

4. Now involve both hands alternately or at the same time; for example, left hand index finger on triangle; two thumbs on circle; right hand little finger on square and left hand little finger on rectangle; left hand middle finger on octagon; right hand ring finger on circle.

FINGER STRENGTHENERS

FOCUS

Discriminating between different pressures
Hand and finger mobility
Finger strengthening

SET-UP

Children make a fist, then release according to the directions given with:

➤ preferred hand

➤ non-preferred hand

➤ both hands

➤ alternate hands

FINGER STRENGTHENERS ACTIVITIES

1. *Directions:*

   ➤ Light fist

   ➤ Hard fist

   ➤ Open quickly

   ➤ Open slowly

   ➤ Open gently

   ➤ Open and stretch flat, hold for 5-second count

   ➤ Close and open quickly repeatedly

   ➤ Press fingers of one hand against fingers of other

   ➤ Interlock fingers and push hands palm outward

   ➤ Extend one arm, fingers up, and let fingers of other hand gently press these extended fingers backward; reverse finger positions and repeat

   ➤ Stand near a wall, facing it. Lean toward wall taking weight on fingers, then bend at elbows until nose just touches wall. Push off wall with fingers until arms are straight. Then lean toward wall again. Continue this front support, alternating hands, and taking weight from hands onto fingers.

FINGER STRENGTHENERS ACTIVITIES *(Continued)*

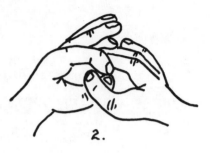

2. *Pincers.* Make a "pincer" by letting thumb and index finger meet. Now interlock thumb and index finger of both hands and try to pull apart. Interlock pincers with a partner's. Can you hold your pincer grip tight without letting your fingers pull apart? Keep repeating with thumb and other fingers.

2.

3. *Hand Squeezers.*

> ➤ Use a "Squellet Ball" or "Sqwish Ball" (available from Sportime).

> ➤ Use cylinder-shaped piece of high-density foam.

> ➤ Use play dough, squeezing it into different shapes.

3.

4. *Scissors, Rock, Paper.* (Played with 2 or more.) Facing players, tap fist of one hand on top of bottom hand, twice, then let hand be a "Rock" (closed fist), or "Paper" (top hand flat on bottom fist), or "Scissors" (index finger and middle finger in a "V" on top of bottom fist). *Rule:* Scissors cut Paper, Rock crushes Scissors, Paper covers Rock. Play to 10 points, or decide on your own scoring system.

PAPER COVERS ROCK!

4.

PALM PLAY

FOCUS

Forearm and wrist mobility

Directionality

SET-UP

➤ Palm up—supernate
➤ Palm down—pronate

PALM PLAY ACTIVITIES

1. Child holds hands out in front, then turns palm up/palm down according to sequence, using:

   ➤ preferred hand

   ➤ non-preferred hand

   ➤ both hands

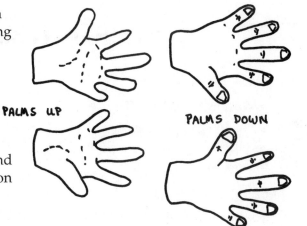

PALMS UP

PALMS DOWN

2. Complete sequences using visual and auditory instruction to train attention and memory:

   ➤ Copy my movements.

   ➤ Copy my movements when I finish showing you.

   ➤ Listen to me and when I finish telling you, do the movement.

   ➤ Hands start in different positions and then begin turning, such as right hand up, left hand up; right hand down, left hand up, etc.

3. Put on *Magic Gloves.* Pretend you are putting on gloves, one at a time. Push the glove on each finger by pressing down along the sides of the thumb and fingers.

4. *Palm Pressing.* Stand facing a partner. One partner has palms up; other partner, palms down with partner's palms touching the others. One partner presses downward, while the other partner presses upward. Reverse roles and repeat.

HAND ROTATORS

FOCUS

| Rotating movements |
| Wrist mobility |
| Hand and finger strength |

SET-UP

Child performs turning motion with hands in the air (mimes actions) with:

➤ preferred hand

➤ non-preferred hand

➤ both hands

HAND ROTATORS ACTIVITIES

1. *Uni-manual.*

   ➤ Turn a tap on or off.

   ➤ Turn a door handle.

2. *Bi-manual.*

   ➤ Turn lid on a jar.

   ➤ Turn tap on and fill a cup with water, then turn tap off.

   ➤ *Bolts, Washers, Nuts.* Use various sized nuts, washers, and bolts. Match correct sized bolt, washer, and nut. Unscrew them all and return to container.

   ➤ Use a screwdriver to screw a nail into a piece of wood.

   ➤ Operate window and door catches or locks.

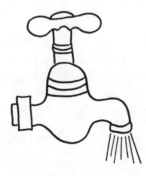

HAND MANIPULATORS

FOCUS

Manipulating movements
Wrist mobility
Hand and finger strength

SET-UP

Child performs manipulating movements with:

➤ preferred hand

➤ non-preferred hand

➤ both hands

HAND MANIPULATORS ACTIVITIES

1. Slide paper clips on 8-1/2″ × 11″ (A4 size) cardboard paper.

2. Place plastic clothespins on an ice cream container.

3. Pin large safety pins into felt or material squares.

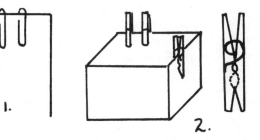

4. Place 12 pegs on a string tied between two chairs. Remove pegs using only one hand. Repeat with the other hand. How many pegs can you collect without dropping any?

5. Stack building blocks or similar objects one on top of each other. Create other ways of stacking the blocks.

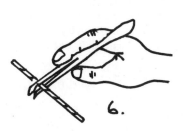

6. Use a pair of tweezers to pick up different objects and place in a container.

HAND MANIPULATORS ACTIVITIES *(Continued)*

7. ***Pass the Cup.*** Divide the class into groups of 4–5 children. Each group stands in a file, one behind the other, and each child has a clothespin. First child holds plastic cup with his or her clothespin. The cup is passed from child to child using only the clothespin. When last child receives the cup, he or she runs to the front of the line with cup and repeats the activity. Continue in this way until each child has taken a turn at running to the front. *Variation:* Use other objects such as straws, stiff cards (such as an old deck of playing cards), ice cream sticks, etc.

8. ***Clothespin Drop.*** Each child will need 10 clothespins and a plastic container such as an ice cream container. Child places container between feet and tries to drop pins, one at a time, from waist height into the container. Child must keep body straight with no bending at the waist. Keep score out of 10 and try again! Repeat dropping pegs from chest height. Repeat dropping pegs from chin level. Vary the type of container and gradually reduce the size of container; for example, from an ice cream container to a margarine container.

9. ***Scavenger Hunt.*** Each child takes an ice cream container and a clothespin to collect a variety of objects from a nearby park or school yard, such as sticks, small stones, twigs, leaves, string, plastic, and so on (no garbage!). Each child then writes the name of each object that he or she has collected on a name card—one card per object. Child then places these name cards face down, spreading them out on a table. Turning one card over at a time, child uses his or her clothespin to select an object out of the container, until all the objects have been selected. Who can do this the quickest? *Variation:* Each container contains the same objects (safety pin, paper clip, pencil, string, straw, coin, etc.) Teacher calls out the name of one object. Using tweezers each child tries to bring his or her object out of the container the quickest!

HAND MANIPULATORS ACTIVITIES *(Continued)*

10. Set up *Hand Manipulator Stations* using the activities and games above. You might set up the stations this way:

    #1—Nuts, Washers & Bolts Challenges; #2—Clothespin Challenges; #3—Safety Pin Challenges; #4—Paper Clip Challenges; #5—Opening and Closing Lids Challenges.

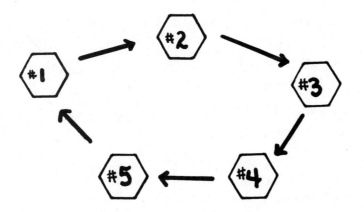

FINGER CLAPPERS, SNAPPERS, AND TAPPERS

FOCUS

Rhythm and timing
Isolation of finger movement
Sequential finger movement
Hand-eye coordination

SET-UP

Providing ample opportunity for children to do rhythmical actions or movement patterns will further enhance their fine-motor abilities. Accompany hand actions with music, drum beats, tambourine, or wooden blocks.

FINGER CLAPPERS, SNAPPERS, AND TAPPERS ACTIVITIES

1. Child follows sequence as set by teacher or another child, such as:

   ➤ hands clap together twice

   ➤ hands clap on desk twice

   ➤ hands clap on knees twice

   Repeat this sequence to music or drum beats.

"CLAPPERS"

2. Child learns to snap fingers. Thumb is pressed on finger pad and is forced off in a sliding movement. Practice this with preferred hand; then other hand; then both hands together.

3. Create different combinations of snapping fingers and clapping hands.

   ➤ Clap–clap; snap–snap

   ➤ Clap–snap; clap–snap

   ➤ Clap–snap right fingers; clap–snap left fingers

4. Pretend you are a *bongo drummer* and clap out different patterns.

   ➤ Use different body parts.

   ➤ Alternate hands; i.e., hit left knee, then right knee.

   ➤ Cross over hands.

"SNAPPERS"

FINGER CLAPPERS, SNAPPERS, AND TAPPERS ACTIVITIES *(Continued)*

5. Create a clapping-finger snapping pattern with a partner.

6. Rest your hand on the desk and tap each finger twice (from 1–5, then 5–1), using

   ➤ preferred hand

   ➤ non-preferred hand

   ➤ both hands together

   ➤ Do this slowly! both hands (alternating)

   "TAPPERS"

7. Repeat activity 6, but change the tapping finger sequence; for example:

   1–1, 3–3, 5–5; 5–5, 3–3,1–1

   1–3–5; 5–3–1

   2–2, 4–4, 1–1, 5–5; 2–4–1–5

8. Go from soft intensity of tap through to hard.

   ➤ Use two fingers together.

   ➤ Start with index finger; keep adding another finger after designated number of taps.

   ➤ Use music to set a rhythm.

9. Create a "finger snap–tap, and clap dance" to your favorite music!

10. *Piano Player.* Child pretends to be playing the piano on the desk, placing one finger down after the other. As the next finger is being placed on the table, the previous one should be lifted. The fingers should be curved but relaxed in the piano-playing position (natural position). The process should be rhythmical.

    Exercises should be carried out with:

    ➤ Preferred hand; non-preferred hand; both hands. Vary the speed from slow to fast.

    ➤ Number fingers. Teacher calls 1, 2, 3, 4, then reverse.

    ➤ Call out numbers in any random order, such as, 3, 5, 1, 4, 2.

    ➤ Vary speed; for example, "1" (slow) then "2, 3" (quick–quick); counting done by teacher; "3, 5" (quick–quick) then "2" (slow).

    ➤ Use the keyboard template shown and have child cut it out and paste onto stiff cardboard. Have child place fingers on the keyboard and "play" different "notes" as shown.

VARIATION:

   ➤ For young children use colored keys instead of letters.

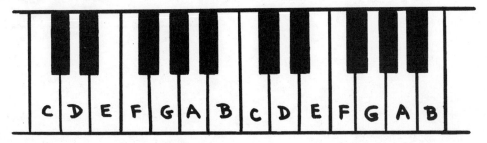

FINGER PAINTING

FOCUS

Isolation of finger movement
Fluency of arm movements
Muscle tension
Hand steadiness

SET-UP

For this activity you will need a variety of jars of different colored washable paint; a large sheet of paper; a paint smock; and a large sheet of plastic spread out on the table. By pressing large sheet of paper onto plastic sheet, you will get your child's *finger painting print.* Put in a suitable place to allow to dry.

Have child use preferred hand; then non-preferred hand according to the following instructions.

FINGER PAINTING ACTIVITIES

1. Start with your pointer finger. Dip your pointer into paint and draw patterns on the plastic sheet.

2. Repeat, using a different finger each time.

3. Repeat, using the other hand.

4. Now create finger patterns using 2 fingers at once; for example: pointer and middle fingers.

5. Create finger patterns using 3 fingers.

6. Create finger patterns using 4 fingers.

7. Create finger patterns using all 5 fingers.

FINGER FLICKING

FOCUS

Opposition
Sequencing
Finger isolation

SET-UP

Child places thumb directly over fingernail and flicks each finger, using:

➤ preferred hand

➤ non-preferred hand

➤ both hands

FINGER FLICKING ACTIVITIES

1. Number fingers 1–5, starting with thumb on right hand. Flick fingers 1–2; 1–3; 1–4; 1–5.

2. Vary intensity from soft to hard flicks.

3. Combine finger flicking, snapping, tapping, and hand clapping to create different rhythm patterns to your favorite music.

4. *Marbles.* Use marbles of different sizes and have child flick them against a wall.

5. *Target Coin Flick.* Take turns with a partner flicking a coin along a table and trying to get it to land in a target area to score points (as shown in the diagram).

6. *Paper Flick Basketball.* Roll up small pieces of paper into a ball and try to flick them into a small garbage bin. Challenge a partner to see who can flick more hoops in 10 tries!

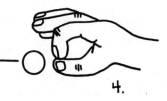

4.

7. Together invent a game, using "flicking" as the main component of the game.

6.

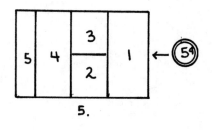

5.

FINGER DIVIDERS

FOCUS

| Isolation of finger movement |
| Sequencing |
| Speed |

SET-UP

Child places hand(s) on desk and moves fingers apart in designated sequence, with:

➤ preferred hand

➤ non-preferred hand

➤ both hands

FINGER DIVIDERS ACTIVITIES

1. All fingers touching, palm down, on desk. Sequence:

   ➤ thumb away, index joins thumb, middle finger, ring finger, and little finger join until all fingers together again

   ➤ index and middle finger together and away from other fingers

   ➤ thumb, index, middle, and ring finger away and return

   ➤ thumb, index, and middle finger away and return

2. Complete finger dividers slowly, but controlled; then quickly, but controlled.

3. *Signing.* Try the following signs:

   "Hang Loose"   "I Love You"

4. *Shadow Fingers.* Use finger dividers to create animal shadows against a wall.

DOG   4.

RABBIT

"Hang Loose"

3.   "I Love You"

30

FINGER DIVIDERS ACTIVITIES *(Continued)*

5. *Scissor Cutting.* Hold hand in the handshake position. Let the pointer finger move up and down in a cutting motion while you say:

➤ "This is the way my scissors cut, scissors cut, scissors cut.

➤ This is the way my scissors cut, so early in the morning!"

Repeat with the other hand. Repeat with both hands at the same time.

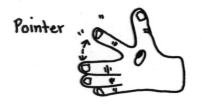

6. *Five Fingers.*

➤ Give me "3!" (show any 3 fingers).

➤ Give me "2!" (show any 2 fingers).

➤ Give me "4!" (show any 4 fingers).

Variation: Use the name of the fingers: "Thumbkin," "Pointer," "Tall man," "Ring man," "Pinky."

7. *Alphabet Signing.* Learn to communicate with the deaf. Some countries use different methods. In Australia and many parts of the world, for example, the two-handed manual alphabet for finger spelling to the sighted deaf is used.

ALPHABET FINGERS

FOCUS

Finger isolation

Association/decoding

SET-UP

Display in large upper-case letters the alphabet with numbers written randomly from 1–5 underneath each letter. Put on posterboard, chalkboard, whiteboard, or transparency. Use two different colors: *Red* for alphabet letter; *Blue* for numbers. Number fingers 1–5: 1—thumb; 2—index; 3—middle; 4—ring; 5—little finger. Child says the letter while raising the indicated finger from a closed fist position, using preferred hand; non-preferred hand; both hands. Here is an example.

A	B	C	D	E	F	G
1	3	2	5	4	4	2
H	I	J	K	L	M	N
3	5	1	4	1	3	5
O	P	Q	R	S	T	U
2	3	5	4	1	1	5
	V	W	X	Y	Z	
	4	3	3	1	2	

VARIATIONS:

➤ Use lower-case letters.

➤ Go from right side to left side for each row.

➤ Mix up the alphabet letters.

➤ Tap appropriate finger on desk while saying the letter.

➤ For young children you can use colors, shapes, or animals to represent fingers. This then becomes a decoding task; for example, red represents the middle finger.

ACTION POEMS AND SONGS

FOCUS

Finger isolation
Manipulation speed
Sequencing actions
Force control

Here are some samples of action poems and songs you can use to further develop finger manipulation skills.

1. **"Eency, Weency, Spider."**

   Eency, weency, spider
   Climbed up the water spout
   Down came the rain
   And washed the spider out!
   Out came the sun
   And dried up all the rain
   So Eency, weency spider
   Climbed up the spout again.

2. **Finger Play.** Paint little faces on your pointer fingers and create a play in which the fingers "talk" to each other.

3. **Hand Climbers.** Sit facing child(ren). In turn have each one place hand on top of another hand. Child whose hand is on the bottom, then places hand on top. Continue in this way.

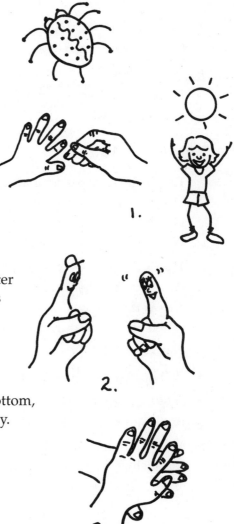

33

4. *Open-Shut; Snap-Snap-Snap.*

Open, shut them; open, shut them—oh so slowly.
Open, shut them; open, shut them—quicker now.
Snap–snap; snap–snap–snap those fingers.

Now do this:
Open, shut; open, shut; snap–snap–snap.
Clap–clap; clap–clap–clap your hands.

Now do all 3 like this:
Open, shut; snap–snap; clap–clap–clap.

Add other actions:

➤ Flick–flick; flick–flick–flick

➤ Tap–tap; tap–tap–tap

➤ Creep–creep; creep–creep–creep

➤ Wiggle–wiggle; shake–shake–shake

➤ Wave "good-bye"–"hello" action

➤ Floppy hands

5. *This Is the Way . . .*

This is the way we scissors cut
Scissors cut, scissors cut.
This is the way we scissors cut
When we are at (our school's name).

This is the way we wave our hands,
Wave our hands, wave our hands.
This is the way we wave our hands,
When we are at (our school's name).

Add other actions:

➤ Roll our hands round and round

➤ Shake our friends' hands

➤ Wash and dry our hands

➤ "Sing" with our hands (like an orchestra conductor)

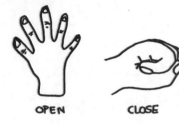

OPEN   CLOSE

SNAP!

FLICK!

TAP!

4.

WAVE

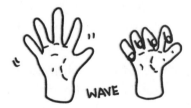

"ROLL"

5.

6. *I'm a Little Piece of Tin.*

I'm a little piece of tin *(pretend to hold a steering wheel of car)*
Nobody knows where I have been *(shake pointer finger; then other)*
Got four wheels and a running board *(show 4 fingers and run on the spot)*
I'm a Chevy—not a Ford! *(thumbs point at self, then hands sweep past each other)*

Honk! Honk! *(squeeze and open hands twice)*

Rattle! Rattle! *(shake all over)*

Crash! Crash! *(slap your legs twice)*

Beep! Beep! *(raise hands high in air and snap fingers)*

Add other actions:

➤ windscreen wipers

➤ signal lights blinking

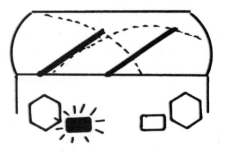

7. Make up your own action song or poem!

SECTION 3

MANIPULATION ACTIVITIES

PRECISION GRIP AND RELEASE

To manipulate objects successfully, children must develop a correct precision grip and timing of the release of the objects. Judgment of object size is also important. There are literally thousands of ideas you can use along the lines of those given here.

FOCUS

Precision grip
Grip release
Fluency of arm transport
Estimation of shape and grip size
Hand steadiness

1. **Match Castles.** Child needs about 30 matches. (**CAUTION:** Remove the heads of the matches.) Have child use preferred hand, then non-preferred hand, to pick up one match at a time and lay carefully in a square pattern as shown. Build up the layers in this way. How high can you construct your castle before it collapses? *Variation:* Use tweezers to pick up matches.

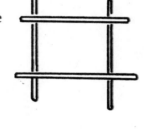

2. **Pick Up Sticks.** You will need a set of "Pick Up Sticks" for this activity. Drop sticks onto the floor or table. In turn, pick up sticks until none are left on the floor. Try not to move any of the other sticks while choosing the one you want to pick up. If you do, you lose a turn. Who will get the most number of sticks?

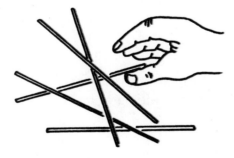

3. ***Spooning.*** Divide class into groups of 4 children. Each group will need 1 teaspoon, 1 tablespoon, a container of dry sand, a container of dry split peas, and a container of uncooked rice. Ask children to bring jars or bottles with different sized neck openings. Encourage them to do this activity carefully so that no spills occur! Children in each group take turns using the large spoon to scoop up sand, peas, and rice into wide necked jars. Then use the small spoons for narrow necked jars. Challenge them to use the tablespoon to place rice, peas, or sand into the narrow necked jars/bottles.

4. ***Tweezers Play.*** Using small objects such as paper clips, safety pins, string, coins, and the like, have child pick them up with tweezers and place in a designated spot (like a container). *Variation:* Draw the objects on a piece of paper and have children use tweezers to pick up the object and place in the correct position.

5. Refer to later in this section on Fine-Motor Boards and Activities for many more precision-grip tasks.

BALANCE FEATHERS

Manipulation activities can be performed with the preferred hand; non-preferred hand; both hands doing the same movement (catching a ball); both hands doing the same movement, but in different directions; both hands involved, but performing different tasks (keystroking).

The development of fine-motor control begins with the development of hand–eye coordination and body management. The following activities have been used to demonstrate how we can begin to bridge the gap between larger body activities and fine-motor control.

Focus

Visual motor control
Arm transport
Finger isolation
Finger dexterity

BALANCE FEATHERS ACTIVITIES

Peacock feathers make ideal "balance feathers." As the feathers are quite fragile, emphasize to child that the feather must be handled with care, in a gentle way. Refer to the Resource Index to find out from where these balance feathers can be purchased.

1. Show me how you can balance your feather in the palm of your favorite hand. What part of the feather must your eyes watch?

   ➤ Balance feather on the back of your hand.

   ➤ Repeat using your other hand.

2. Show me how you can balance the feather just on your pointer finger. Now try to balance it on each of the other fingers: middle finger; ring finger; pinkie; and thumb.

   ➤ Repeat using your other hand.

41

BALANCE FEATHERS ACTIVITIES *(Continued)*

3. Transfer your balance feather from hand to hand.

4. Show me how you can balance your feather on other body parts: nose; forehead; shoulder; elbow; foot.

4.

5. Try to transfer the feather to different body parts.

6. Now try to balance your feather while slowly moving forward; bending down and then straightening up; moving around in a circle; touching an object or wall or another body part.

7. Create a feather balancing stunt of your own!

6.

VARIATIONS:

➤ Substitute balance feathers for "balance sticks" which are pieces of wooden dowels cut into 60–90 cm (2–3 ft) lengths and 6 mm (1/4 inch) in diameter.

Variations

7.

FLOATING SCARVES

A floating scarf is a lightweight nylon square 45 × 60 cm (16″ × 24″). These scarves will float in the air almost in slow motion, making it easy for the child to visually track. Also, because the scarves move slowly, the child has time to prepare and estimate grip. The scarves are particularly good for promoting timing of release.

FOCUS

Hand-eye coordination
Hand mobility and transport
Fluency of arm transport
Grip release
Sequencing

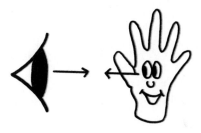

FLOATING SCARVES ACTIVITIES

1. Put your scarf over a knee and grab it in the middle with your first three fingers of your favorite hand. This is called the "pincer grip." Wave your scarf through the air as if it were a "ghost."

2. Toss your scarf upwards and let it settle down on a different body part each time. Toss with one hand; then toss with the other hand.

3. Toss your scarf upward and wait as long as you can to grab it downward before it touches the floor. Repeat using the other hand.

4. Let your scarf travel around your waist; through your legs in a figure-8; and so on.

FLOATING SCARVES ACTIVITIES *(Continued)*

5. Toss your scarf across your body and let the other hand grab it with a downward "clawing-like" action.

6. Show me what other tasks you can do with your scarf.

7. *Challenge:* Start by holding two scarves in one hand. Then toss one, toss the other—keep this pattern going!

8. **Partner Toss.** At the same time toss your scarves back and forth to each other.

VARIATIONS FOR TWO SCARVES:

➤ Toss both scarves in the air at the same time, then try to catch them.

➤ Try to juggle with two scarves by tossing one across the body; then at the peak of the first scarf, toss the second scarf. Grab downward with the hand on that side. Cues: "Toss-toss, grab-grab."

Variations – Two Scarves

BALLOON PLAY

FOCUS

Visual tracking
Finger dexterity
Arm transport
Hand-eye coordination
Foot-eye coordination

BALLOON PLAY ACTIVITIES

Balloons, like floating scarves, move in slow motion and are easy to track. Balloons are inexpensive and come in a variety of colors, sizes, and shapes. For a younger child, start with a bigger balloon, then gradually reduce the size as skill level improves.

1. Blow up a balloon, then let it go. Track it with eyes as it zooms around the room. Blow up balloon again and tie a knot in the top.

2. Keep your balloon afloat by gently tapping it with the body part I call out. Don't let it touch the floor: right pointer finger, left foot; knees; head and pinkies, left and then right elbows.

3. Use a lummi stick to keep your balloon floating in the air. Tap with either hand. (See "Lummi Stick Fun" later in this section.)

4. Hold the balloon in the air with your feet!

5. Keep the balloon in the air using only your feet while in the sitting or lying position.

45

BALLOON PLAY ACTIVITIES *(Continued)*

6. Call out which body part is to be used to tap the balloon: right pointer finger; left foot; right shoulder; left elbow; right knee; head. *Variation:* Try combinations such as: head and knee; elbow and foot; head–knee–foot.

7. Partner activities:

   ➤ Tap balloon in turn using only one body part; tap using a different body part each time.

   ➤ Sit on chairs facing each other, about 2 m apart. Tap balloon toward each other trying to force balloon over partner's head.

   ➤ Each partner holds a lummi stick, trying to keep balloon afloat by gently tapping balloon.

   ➤ Balance a balloon with your partner by holding it between your heads—no hands allowed! Explore other ways of balancing the balloon.

   ➤ Invent a game of your own with your partner!

DECK RING PLAY

FOCUS

Hand-eye coordination
Visual tracking
Grip release
Foot-eye coordination

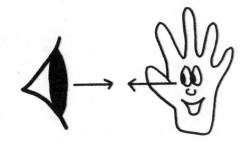

DECK RING PLAY ACTIVITIES

Deck rings are rubber throwing rings, available in "rainbow" colors. Deck ring activities help to develop hand–eye coordination, foot–eye coordination, and object control.

1. Place deck ring on your head; walk forward, backward, sideways; kneel, sit down, then stand up; turn around.

2. Show me how you can spin the deck ring on the floor. Use your favorite hand; use your other hand. *Variations:* Run to touch an object and grab your ring before it stops spinning. Now try to touch two objects!

3. Show me how you can flip the deck ring in the air and catch it. Use both hands; then one hand.

4. Put the deck ring flat on the ground or floor. Try to pick it up with one foot and flip it into your hands. Repeat using the other foot.

5. In sitting position, place the ring vertically or "standing tall" between your feet. Rock gently backward onto your back and try to hold the ring with your feet, keeping legs straight.

DECK RING PLAY ACTIVITIES *(Continued)*

6. Toss deck ring upward using your favorite hand and catch it in both hands; catch it in your favorite hand. *Variations:* Toss deck ring with your other hand; catch it in both hands; then catch it in favorite hand.

7. Toss deck ring up in the air, clap your hands once, and catch. Repeat, clapping hands twice, catch. Continue this pattern. Repeat snapping your fingers.

8. Toss deck ring with one hand, and catch it in the other.

9. Roll your deck ring like a tire along the floor. Can you keep it moving? Change its direction from time to time.

10. Roll the deck ring along the floor. Run after it and try to get in front to grab it in one or both hands.

11. Now try to hook it with one of your feet. Try hooking the ring with your other foot as it rolls along!

12. Toss one deck ring back and forth with a partner. Use a two-hand catch, then just a one-hand catch.

VARIATIONS:

➤ Partners each have a lummi stick. Use lummi stick to send the ring back and forth to each other; along the floor; in the air.

➤ Invent another game using the deck ring and lummi stick.

LUMMI STICK FUN

Lummi sticks (dowel sticks, happy sticks) when used with music are a novel way of promoting fine-motor control. The following manipulation activities can be performed with the preferred hand; non-preferred hand; both hands doing the same movement (catching a ball); both hands doing the same movement, but in different directions; both hands involved, but performing different tasks.

A lummi stick can be made from 25 mm (1 inch) doweling cut into a 30-cm (12-inch) length. Create 2 sticks for each child and for yourself. Child could personalize the lummi stick by painting it. Choose your own music that has a distinctive beat.

FOCUS

Hand-eye coordination
Finger isolation
Force control
Fluency of arm transport
Bilateral coordination
Hand dexterity and rhythm

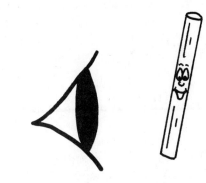

LUMMI STICK FUN ACTIVITIES

1. *Passing.* Hold your lummi stick straight up (vertically). Pass your stick back and forth from hand to hand. Do this with your eyes closed. Pass stick around your belly button; knees; ankles. Pass stick around one leg through the middle, and around the other leg (figure-8).

2. *Spinning.* Show me how you can spin your lummi stick on the floor using your favorite hand; using your other hand. Spin two sticks at same time.

LUMMI STICK FUN ACTIVITIES *(Continued)*

3. **Flipping.** Holding one end of the stick, flip it over once, trying to catch it at the same end. Try this with each hand. *Variation:* Flip stick from one hand to the other hand.

4. **Hammering.** Using two sticks, let one be the hammer; the other, the nail. Tap stick "through" your hand. Switch hand roles and repeat.

5. **Punching.** Hold lummi sticks as shown in a palms-down grip and carefully punch ends to slide sticks until hands touch. Turn hands to a palms-up grip and repeat.

6. **Rhythm Sticks.** Explore tapping out different rhythms using one stick, then two sticks. Using favorite music, tap out rhythm patterns. (Use directional language such as: 2 taps to right side, 2 taps to left side; 2 taps in front.)

7. **Climbing.** Show me how you can make your fingers climb the stick, then climb back down. Do this with your other hand. Do this with your eyes shut. Climb with your fingers, not your hand!

8. **Rolling.** Place the stick on the ground. Roll it away with your fingers; roll it toward you. Do this several times, then repeat using your other hand.

9. **Twirling.** Can you twirl your lummi stick as if it were a baton?

10. **Balloon Tapping.** Using a lummi stick, tap the balloon to keep it up in the air. Use your favorite hand; use your other hand. Tap the balloon back and forth with a partner.

PLASTICINE/PLAY DOUGH

Plasticine and play dough are excellent for promoting force control and spatial aspects, and for strengthening small fingers.

Purchase commercial plasticine or make your own play dough using the following ingredients: 2 cups flour; 2 cups water; 1 cup salt; 2 tablespoons cream of tartar; 2 tablespoons oil; food coloring. Mix all ingredients in a saucepan. Cook on low heat, stirring mixture until it hardens and is no longer sticky. Remove from heat, cool, and roll into balls. Store in airtight container and refrigerate. Children can use a variety of cutting tools, such as cookie cutter shapes, egg cups, rolling pin, and so on.

FOCUS

Muscle tone
Finger manipulation
Force control
Muscle tension

PLASTICINE/PLAY DOUGH ACTIVITIES

1. Use both hands to roll dough/plasticine into a ball.

2. Use both hands to roll ball on table into a long thin "snake."

3. Other things children can do:
   - ➤ squishing
   - ➤ flattening with a rolling pin
   - ➤ using cookie cutter to make different shapes

4. Roll into long, thin strips and cut with safety knife or scissors.

5. Roll these smaller pieces to create numbers or letters. Make your own name or initials.

6. Practice "cutting" using long strips of plasticine or play dough.

7. Cut the dough using safety scissors.

8. Cut the dough using a knife and fork.

51

SORTING/FEELING

Essential to developing accurate manipulative skills is tactile and kinesthetic feedback. Without sensitivity in these areas, the child lacks the ability to accurately refine movements. The child should be exposed to objects varying in texture, size, weight, and shape.

FOCUS

Tactile stimulation/sensitivity
Finger control
Kinesthetic sense
Speed of manipulation

SORTING/FEELING ACTIVITIES

1. ***Card Sorting.*** You need a deck of playing cards.

   ➤ Teach child to "shuffle" cards. Start with half a pack.

   ➤ Sort cards into reds and blacks.

   ➤ Sort cards into suits.

   ➤ Sort each suit into order: Ace, King, Queen, Jack, 10, 9, 8, 7, 6, 5, 4, 3, 2.

   Invent your own way to sort cards; for example, put cards into a pile with one card face up, the other card face down.

2. ***Object Sorting.*** In a container, put a variety of objects such as paper clips, buttons, safety pins, bottle tops, nickels, marbles, playing chips, and so on.

   ➤ Use your "pincer" grip (thumb and pointer) to sort like objects into the same pile.

   ➤ How quickly can you do this?

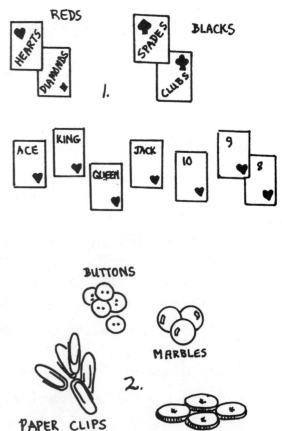

52

SORTING/FEELING ACTIVITIES *(Continued)*

3. *Feelies.* Put several objects in a shoe box, such as spoon, comb, pencil, ruler, eraser, fork, variety of material, clothespin, soap, coin, and so on. Blindfold child as he or she sits on a chair near the box.

   ➤ Reach into box, feel object, describe object (long, soft, hard, cold . . .), then name it.

   ➤ How many will you guess right?

   ➤ Place objects of different heights in the box and ask child to group or sequence according to height.

   ➤ Repeat using different shapes and textures.

   ➤ Draw objects they feel.

   ➤ Feel different angled slopes simultaneously with both hands and ask child to identify the steepest slope. *(kinesthetic sensitivity)*

   ➤ Place a number of familiar objects in child's hand and ask him or her to memorize the items.

   ➤ To add difficulty to the task, ask child to remember objects in the correct order, or take the blindfold off and ask child to place objects in the correct order. Try this challenge with geometric or letter shapes.

4. *Alternative Feelie Box Design.* Some children feel insecure when blindfolded; therefore, another kinesthetic alternative is required. Take a cardboard box, cut out along one side, and secure a curtain across the opening.

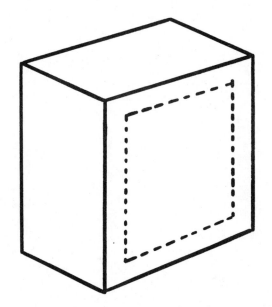

SORTING/FEELING ACTIVITIES *(Continued)*

5. ***Guess the Object.*** Divide children into 3 groups. Each group has a towel with 12 objects—such as a hairbrush, pencil, jar lid, spoon, fork, coin, button, marble, shell, bead, toothbrush, spool of thread, candle—hidden underneath the towel. In turn, child places hand under towel, feels the object, and tries to guess what it is. He or she then takes out the object, shows it to the other two members of the group, and places the object back under the towel. Continue the task in this way.

6. ***Tactile Box Challenge.*** Create a tactile box with textures. Match items only by feel.

THREADING/BRAIDING/LACING

There are many stimulating activities available to challenge young children. Many of these activities are "lifestyle activities" such as dressing, shoelace tying, and handling eating utensils (using plasticine as pretend food). These are important skills to practice along with similar activities described here.

FOCUS

Bi-manual control
Precision grip
Dexterity
Hand-eye coordination

THREADING/BRAIDING/LACING ACTIVITIES

1. *Macaroni Necklace.* Use colored macaroni and strong string or a thin shoelace. Attach a paper clip to one end, and use the other end for threading macaroni pieces onto string. Make your necklace interesting by using different color sequences. Knot end of thread together to form a necklace. Create another one.

2. *Straw Necklace.* Use different colored plastic straws cut into 3-cm lengths and a shoelace or string with a clothespin clipped onto string at one end. Thread straws in a color sequence pattern, such as yellow–red–blue–green, to create a bright necklace. Create a name bracelet.

THREADING/BRAIDING/LACING ACTIVITIES
(Continued)

3. **Lacing.** Create different lacing cards using a hole puncher. Have child thread string through holes to make different lacing patterns.

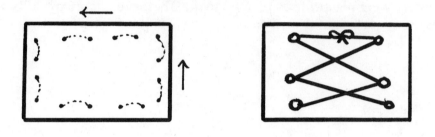

4. **Braiding or Plaiting.** Use material such as thick wool, ribbons, thick cord, or strips of material. Attach three different colored strips of material (if possible) into a support, such as a piece of cardboard. Teach child how to braid.

5. **Paper Chains.** Each child has several strips of paper 2 cm × 10 cm (1″ × 4″). Join the ends of a strip by gluing, taping, or stapling together. Continue to add another link in this way. Join all the children's chains together to form one long chain. Use to decorate your room or a holiday tree.

6. **Laced Name Plates.** For each child you will need one piece of cardboard 15 cm × 15 cm (6″ × 6″), one large darning needle, one pencil, some colored wool, and masking tape. Have each child draw his or her initials on the card in large letters. Use the darning needle to carefully prick holes along each letter, about 12 mm (1/2″) apart. (See example shown.) Then thread the 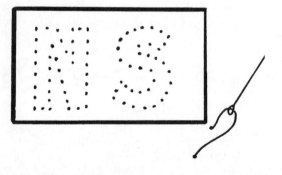 darning needle with wool and tie a knot in one end. Now lace the wool through the holes starting from the back of the card, to the front, then to the back. Continue this pattern until finished and tape wool to the back of card. Now you have your own personalized "license plate"!

THREADING/BRAIDING/LACING ACTIVITIES
(Continued)

7. ***Checkered Place Mat.*** For each child you will need two different colored squares of paper 20 cm × 20 cm (8″ × 8″), scissors, and glue. Prepare one square sheet by marking a dotted fold line through the center and vertical lines drawn 25 mm (1″) apart and from the three edges as shown. Photocopy this so that each child will have a copy of the pattern.

On the second square sheet draw 25 mm (1″) strips and photocopy, one for each child.

Have each child fold the first square sheet in half and cut along the lines drawn. Then cut the second square sheet into the 25 mm (1″) strips. Now unfold the first square sheet and lay it flat. Starting from the back, weave the first strip under and over, ending on the back. Start the next strip from the front and weave under and over. Weave the third strip from the back. Continue this pattern. Glue ends to secure in place.

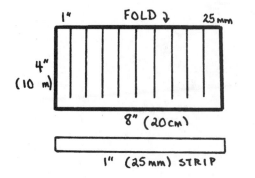

PATTERN

MANIPULATION GAMES

1. ***Shoe Scramble.*** Form groups of 4 children and have them stand in file formation behind a starting line, each group spaced evenly apart in front of a marker. Each member of the group removes his or her shoes and puts them in a pile 5 meters (15 feet) from the start marker. Ideally, each child should have laced shoes.

On signal "Shoe scramble," each player in turn runs to the pile of shoes, finds his or her own pair, returns to the end of his or her group, puts on shoes, and ties them. As soon as this player reaches the end of the line, the next player runs forward to find his or her shoes. Continue in this way. Which group will complete the task the quickest? Form new groups and repeat the challenge.

I.

MANIPULATION GAMES *(Continued)*

2. ***Knots.*** Form groups of 3 children, each child with a piece of standard rope that is 25 mm (1") in diameter and 60 cm (2 feet) in length. Have children practice tying different knots, such as half-hitch knot and reef knot. Ask each group to design a creative knot of its own. Teach this knot to another group. See the illustrations for examples.

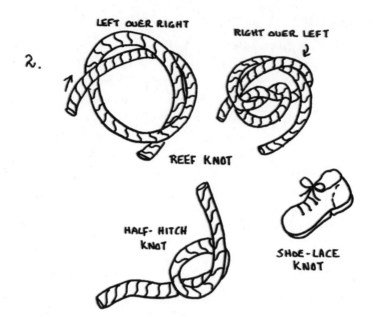

LEFT OVER RIGHT

RIGHT OVER LEFT

REEF KNOT

HALF-HITCH KNOT

SHOE-LACE KNOT

3. ***Pipe Cleaner Play.*** Use pipe cleaners to make different constructions. Use your imagination!

PIPE CLEANER CAT

PIPE CLEANER PERSON

KEYSTROKING

Focus

Finger isolation
Bi-manual dexterity
Hand-eye coordination
Manipulative speed

Today's young children will become a generation of computer-literate whiz-kids, in which computer technology will be more and more a part of their everyday life—and at an earlier age! The basic skill of "keystroking" is a fine-motor bi-manual skill.

Keystroking while screen watching (which is a kinesthetic ability or the ability to make positional changes without the aid of vision) will be the required skill for years to come. Here are some activities you can do with your child at an early age to develop the skills he or she will need to become "keystroke" efficient. If possible, try to obtain a few old keyboards for station work.

KEYSTROKING ACTIVITIES

1. Reproduce a keyboard layout on posterboard or use the keyboard pattern provided. Enlarge the keyboard pattern on the photocopier to real size and glue onto a piece of cardboard. The "Home" hand position is the middle row of the keyboard as shown. Have child trace the keyboard onto another piece of paper and color in the "Home" keys.

2. Now have child position his or her right hand on the keyboard. Let's learn the first four letters in the "Home" position: Pointer—**J**, Middle—**K**, Ring finger—**L**, Pinkie—**;**.

3. Position the left hand on the "Home" keys. Pointer—**F**, Middle—**D**, Ring finger—**S**, Pinkie—**A**.

4. Now have child position both hands on the "Home" keys and practice keystroking these eight characters by your calling out letters and having child tap the appropriate letter. Keep practicing. Then have child tap the letters while keeping eyes closed.

5. Let's learn the next two keys: **H** and **G**. Use the pointer finger of your right hand to tap **H**; use the pointer finger of your left hand to tap **G**. Practice keystroking these letters. Practice with your eyes closed.

6. "Pinkies" are used for the **SHIFT** keys. You can create an upper-case letter by pressing **SHIFT-letter** (hold down shift key while pressing the desired letter). Practice.

7. Repeat these activities using the keyboard pad. Child watches the screen while typing a given letter, instead of closing eyes. Continue in this way to learn all the "key" positions on the keyboard.

8. Now practice pointing and clicking with the "mouse."

9. *Variation:* Learn to play a musical instrument such as a recorder, flute, or guitar!

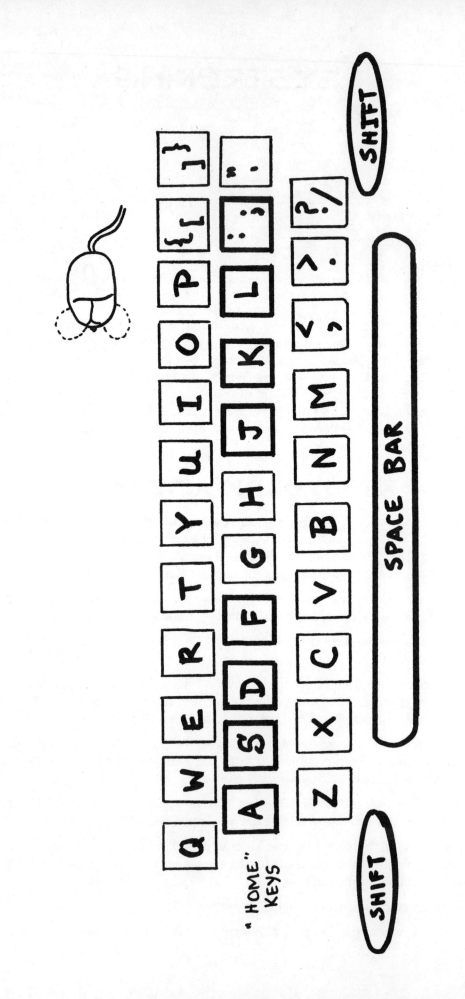

KEYBOARD PATTERN

FINE-MOTOR BOARDS AND ACTIVITIES

In these fine-motor circuits, the children are presented with bi-manual and uni-manual tasks. The children initially work at their own pace for a set period of time with the emphasis being on the correct body movements when manipulating. Once the children are demonstrating correct movements, the tasks can be made more demanding by placing time constraints on the activities and having the children complete the task as quickly as possible (for example, ask child to stack 10 blocks as quickly as possible; record the time taken to complete the task), or by seeing how many items can be completed within a time constraint (for example, how many beads can be threaded in 90 seconds; the number is recorded).

The items you use in these circuits are dependent only upon your imagination and availability of some simple and inexpensive resources. Blocks, straws, pegs, rice and tweezers, marbles, pipe cleaners, nuts and bolts, Lego™ and other building activities as well as some aspects of commercial games can be used in the circuits. Circuits also allow you to introduce cognitive aspects into the manipulative tasks, with the difficulty of the cognitive task dependent upon the child's developmental level. This has the purpose of extending the manipulative skill in a controlled situation and challenging the children to complete the task while concentrating on other aspects and concepts. Second, it allows the children to complete learning tasks using a medium other than pencil and paper.

The following concepts are very useful to reinforce both auditory and visual ability using fine-motor circuits:

- ➤ colors
- ➤ shapes
- ➤ letters (alphabet)
- ➤ words
- ➤ mathematics
- ➤ decoding skills
- ➤ memory skills
- ➤ sequencing

Example: Take some simple connectable colored blocks and work through the above concepts.

COLOR

Children connect the colored blocks in the correct order by following a pattern on a piece of paper or listening to instructions on a tape recorder. They have to recognize colors and sequence the blocks using auditory or visual input.

Shapes and Decoding

Again using visual or auditory input, children are exposed to different colored shapes on a sheet of paper. The children have to join a determined number of blocks together and place them on the designated shape. By introducing the concept of placing a certain number or color of blocks on a particular shape, we are introducing decoding skills. For example:

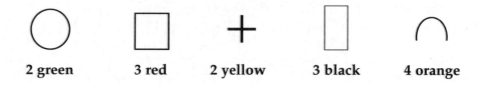

| 2 green | 3 red | 2 yellow | 3 black | 4 orange |

Another shapes and decoding activity is to repeat this pattern in a different order down the page without the numbers underneath.

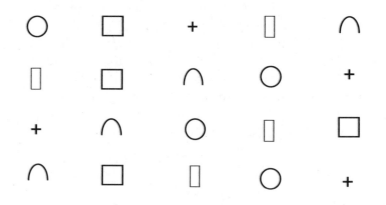

Put on a standard 8-1/2″ × 11″ sheet of paper.

Letters and Numbers

Draw letters on the blocks. Have children complete the alphabet or follow auditory or visual instructions to complete blocks of particular letters (requiring visual and/or auditory selective attention and memory). A similar concept can be followed using numbers.

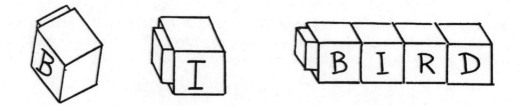

WORDS AND MATH

The next stage is to ask the children to make words using the blocks with letters written on them. A similar concept is completing simple math tasks using the blocks with numbers on them.

MEMORY

As described in the activities on the previous page, using a tape recorder and manipulative tasks is an excellent means of promoting auditory memory. For example:

> "I'm going to ask you to do some tasks for me so listen very carefully. Wait until I have finished telling you your tasks and when I say 'Go' I want you to do all the things I told you. Remember, listen carefully and start when I say 'Go.' Join the red and yellow block together, and place the blue block in the square. Go!"

You can gradually increase the number of tasks and then require the children to complete the tasks in the correct sequence.

Tip: The fine-motor task can be made more difficult by having the children use implements, such as tweezers, to manipulate the objects.

EXAMPLES OF CIRCUIT BOARDS

The following pages provide a number of ideas for creating circuit boards. These boards can be easily made, but can also be purchased commercially; most of the examples still incorporate the cognitive aspects described earlier.

Note: All the boards have adjustable Formica® or cardboard tabs on which the words, letters, numbers, colors, or shapes are written. The tabs are held on the board with Velcro™ dots. Some of the activities can use manipulative equipment, such as tweezers and chopsticks, once mastery with the fingers has been achieved.

CARDBOARD TAB

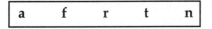

EXAMPLE 1

a	f	r	t	n
●	●	●	●	●
s	q	w	o	p
●	●	●	●	●
c	l	v	m	j
●	●	●	●	●
s	n	z	b	u
●	●	●	●	●
x	y	k	d	I
●	●	●	●	●

The type of board represented above can take the following form:

➤ nails and twine

➤ holes and pegs

➤ nuts and bolts (nuts are glued to the board)

With these boards a number of variations of the different types of manipulation can be used (uni-manual right and left handed; bi-manual). Threading activities are not recommended on the large board represented above.

EXAMPLE 2

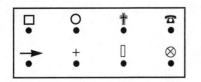

This is an example of a threading board using shapes. Once again, this has Velcro™ adjustable tabs.

EXAMPLES OF CIRCUIT BOARDS *(Continued)*

EXAMPLE 3

A box with no top or bottom is made with allowance for tabs along the top edge of the box. Holes are drilled along the top edge so that threading, nuts and bolts, as well as clothespins can be used as the method of manipulation.

EXAMPLE 4

Use boxes or any other container with different size holes or slits in which to place objects. Objects of varying size and shape (for example, marbles, buttons, rice, and beads) can be manipulated using the fingers, tweezers, chopsticks, or any other manipulative tool.

EXAMPLE 5

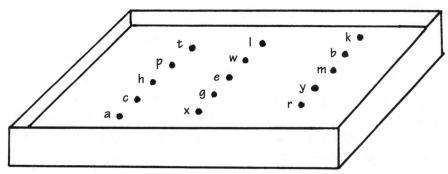

In this example, the bottom of the container is plastic so that colored water can be placed on the dots with an eye dropper, or small items can be placed on the dots with tweezers.

EXAMPLE 6

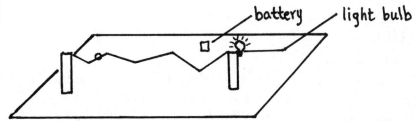

Set up a simple circuit with different shaped wire patterns and different sized implements for tracing. Circuit wire design needs to be horizontal as well as vertical.

EXAMPLES OF CIRCUIT BOARDS *(Continued)*

EXAMPLE 7

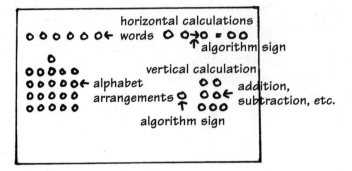

The alphabet board can be used for alphabets, numbers, words, and calculations. Blocks have to be prepared with letters and numbers on them. (For mathematics, 1-cm [1/2-inch] cubes are ideal.) Manipulation can again be with fingers, tweezers, and similar manipulation tools.

EXAMPLE 8

This small board can be used for many speed tasks. The board must be accompanied by small dowel pegs 2 cm (1 inch) in length or burned matches. The dowel pegs are painted red at one end and green at the other (or any two other combinations). The task is to either move rows down or invert the pegs.

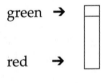

EXAMPLE 9

Snakes and Ladders board

Find an inexpensive "Snakes and Ladders" board and glue it onto some plywood. Drill holes in the middle of each square and add twine. The children can move pegs or thread their way up the board.

EXAMPLES OF CIRCUIT BOARDS *(Continued)*

EXAMPLE 10

	og	ig	ug	ell	uck	ing	in	op
d								
m								
s								
t								
p								

In this example, a grid is made on the board so that matchings and word constructions can be made. For example, to combine **s** with "og, ig, ug," etc., the child places a peg in these grid places. This is an ideal challenge for spatial aspects. Small holes should be drilled.

EXAMPLE 11

1	2	3	4	5	6
●	●	●	●	●	●
1	4	2	5	3	5
●	●	●	●	●	●
3	5	6	1	4	2
●	●	●	●	●	●

CODE (colors matched against numbers)

Wherever there is a 1, the child must place a red peg; 2, a green peg, etc. Use numbers, letters, shapes, etc. On each row present the colors, shapes, letters, etc., in a different order so that the child must decode the pattern.

OTHER USEFUL ITEMS

➤ Purchase nuts and bolts of all sizes. Use some with heads that require manipulation with a normal screwdriver, some requiring a wrench.

➤ Use many colored pegs, at least 6 lots of 6 different colors, for decoding tasks alone. The commercial plastic ones are fine or you may wish to make pegs from the thinnest dowel, 3 cm (1.2 inches) long and the tip painted.

➤ Include commercial games (dependent on availability and budget) that lend themselves to circuits, such as "Beadbugs,™" "Jenga,™" "Lego,™" "Mechano,™" "Pick Up Sticks,™" "Ping Pong,™" "Tip It,™" "Spirograph,™" as well as template activities.

➤ Use stacking items such as cards and dominoes.

➤ Make or purchase plasticine and play dough.

MANIPULO BOARD

This manipulative aid can be made very quickly and economically, has multiple uses, and takes up little space in a child's desk or tray.

DESCRIPTION

The manipulo board is best made from three ply board, the dimensions being approximately 20 cm (8 inches) by 10 cm (4 inches). The board has 26 holes drilled through it just large enough to allow a matchstick to fit in the hole. In the bottom middle, another small hole is drilled that has a length of plastic thread attached to it. The front side of the board has the alphabet randomly written on it so that one letter is above each hole. On the other side, the numbers 0–23 are randomly written above the holes with a +, ÷, ×, and − symbols above the four corner holes.

(FRONT)

●	●	●	●	●	●	●
e	u	t	y	f	a	p
●	●	●	●	●	●	●
j	b	g	z	m	o	w
●	●	●	●	●	●	●
c	v	n	l	i	x	d
●	●	●	●	●	●	●
	h	k	q	r	s	
		●				

(BACK)

+						−
●	●	●	●	●	●	●
	2	5	11	20	13	22
●	●	●	●	●	●	●
7	15	3	4	17	0	8
●	●	●	●	●	●	●
16	1	12	6	14	19	22
●	●	●	●	●	●	●
÷	9	10	18	21	23	x
●						●

The manipulative items required for the board are thread (thin plastic tube is ideal because it does not tangle easily) and blackened matches. (These can be kept in a film container.) With careful placement, beads or marbles can be placed on the holes.

Tip: A small hole can be placed in the top of the container so the children can place their matches in through the hole.

MANIPULO BOARD ACTIVITIES

The manipulo board is set up for uni-manual and bi-manual tasks in isolation or while completing cognitive tasks. Why use this board for cognitive tasks? It provides an alternative way to always using pencil and paper as the medium. For children who are experiencing writing difficulties, this can provide a welcome relief.

1. Simple threading.

2. Match placement, using preferred hand, non-preferred hand, or two hands simultaneously.

3. Place one or two rows of matches in the board and move the rows downward, upward, sideways, to the left, or to the right.

4. Place the matches in all the holes with the blackened side up. Using one hand only, take the match out, reverse it, and place it back in the hole.

5. Sequence the alphabet or numbers. Thread or place matches in the appropriate holes. If you actually want to test alphabet knowledge, cover several letters so that the child does not simply fill all the holes.

6. Make words using threading or match placement.

7. Do simple calculations using threading or matches, e.g., 6 + 8. The child threads the number "6," then threads the "+" sign, then the number "8," and finally the answer. Or the child simply threads the answers to a series of mental mathematics problems.

8. Using matches, the two numbers to be added are represented with matches with the head (black side) up, and the sign and answer represented with the bottom up.

9. Following instructions to promote directional language, the child places a match head up in the top right corner of the board, then places a match bottom up in the third hole from the left in the second row.

10. *Memory training.* Use similar instructions as above, but do not allow the child to commence until all the instructions are given.

SECTION 4

PENCIL-AND-PAPER ACTIVITIES

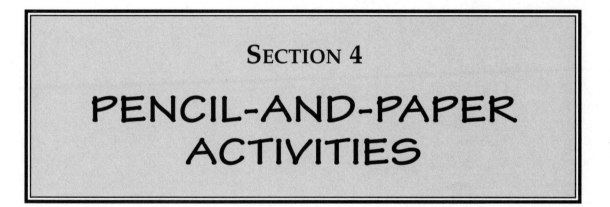

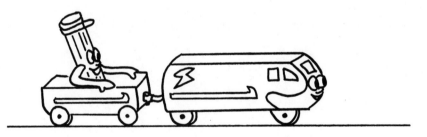

PENCIL-AND-PAPER ACTIVITIES

Before commencing this section, become familiar with the aspects of posture, grip, and pencil control discussed in Section 5 on handwriting. Once the children are introduced to writing implements, they should also be introduced to correct writing techniques even though they are not yet completing formal handwriting. To ignore this aspect will mean the development of poor techniques that quickly become habitual and difficult to correct.

The following activities are simply examples of ideas that you need to develop with children. The reproducible blackline masters are excellent for obtaining and reproducing shapes and pictures that can then be adapted to the guidelines discussed below.

PENCIL ACTIVITY GOALS

1. Promote correct posture to not only enhance pencil skills but to physically prevent back and visual strain.

2. Promote effective grip.

3. Ensure all children have the prerequisite perceptual abilities.

4. Promote form and fluency through good developmental teaching and practice.

5. Provide children with the appropriate language skills.

6. Monitor and improve muscle tone so that excessive tension does not occur.

7. Promote pencil control through correct temporal and spatial movements among the hand, shoulder, and arm.

    Note: Allowing children to finger paint is useful for the first stages in all the activities. Utensil control can then follow. Drawing will be an ongoing process, the complexity of the drawings dependent upon the developmental level of the child.

SEQUENTIAL ORDER OF PENCIL ACTIVITIES

1. Scribble
2. Color
3. Channel
4. Trace
5. Copy

SCRIBBLING

Scribbling is important for developing fluent and relaxed movements and establishing basic patterns. You may want to have the child complete finger-painting scribbling patterns before moving onto writing implements. Start with random scribbles emphasizing fluency and relaxation, and then move onto the following activities. Remember, the fluent action is important at this stage rather than an accurate reproduction of the example scribble.

Tip: An empty roll-on deodorant bottle filled with paint also allows for fluent movements.

SCRIBBLING ACTIVITIES

Create these scribbling patterns. For each pattern, have the child initially alternate between pressing very hard to pressing lightly so that the child experiences the difference. This experimentation can assist in guiding the child toward the correct writing pressure.

1. Keeping your pencil on the paper, draw continuous lines. Lines must not touch! (One is done for you.)

2. Draw "angry" lines—zigzags from left right along the paper.

3. Draw wavy "happy" lines from left to right along your paper.

4. Draw a continuous squiggly line pattern over the paper. Start on the left side and do not let your pencil go off the paper!

5. Try drawing these scribble patterns. Create some scribble pictures of your own, too!

1.

2. ANGRY

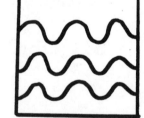

3. HAPPY

5.

4. SQUIGGLES

MORE ADVANCED SCRIBBLING ACTIVITIES

Child now uses crayons, colored marking pens, or colored pencils to create the following patterns on a large sheet of drawing paper.

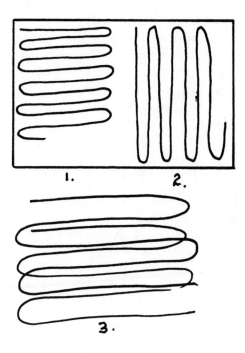

1. Draw pattern from left to right.

2. Draw pattern from top to bottom.

3. Repeat #1 and #2 holding two pens (pencils) at once.

4. Draw patterns within the pattern.

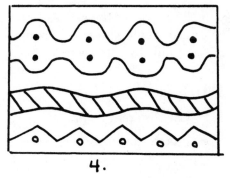

5. Draw a pattern and write your name or numbers within the pattern.

6. Draw a pattern and color in the sections.

7. Create a "scribble critter" and give it a name!

6.

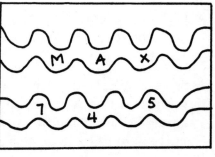

5.

COLORING

The coloring book is a multi-purpose resource. All developmental paper activities—with the exception of scribbling—can be completed using this resource. The progressive development is to have the children initially color in the picture. Next they trace around the outline of the picture or reproduce it using tracing paper. The children can then be asked to copy simple parts of the picture and then draw a similar picture of their own.

But there's more! The next stage is for the children to draw an outline around the picture, which they then tear around with their fingers. Finally, the children can complete the task, cutting as accurately as possible around the picture. Not bad from one picture!

COLORING SEQUENCE

1. Random coloring to promote fluent arm transport and hand movements.

2. Simple open shapes that require straight strokes and allow large hand movements. Emphasize to the child that he or she should use all horizontal or vertical strokes to make it appear even.

3. Simple open shapes that require moving around curves.

4. Increasing complexity with compartments, differing angles, and curves.

5. The sizes of the spaces to be colored continue to be reduced, therefore demanding more control. Too hard too soon creates problems of failure from the beginning.

TIPS:

➤ Use different colors.

➤ Practice using different angles of strokes: horizontal, vertical, slants.

➤ Remember to try to emphasize the spatial aspects of coloring; that is, inside the lines!

➤ Start with pictures that allow larger hand movements, e.g., shapes, and gradually introduce pictures of increasing complexity.

Many examples and samples showing progressive development through the paper and pencil activities now follow. They provide guidelines for the teachers as to the "what" and the "when" to teach through Pencil-and-Paper Activities. These full-page masters can be reproduced for individual or small group use.

Name _____

SEQUENTIAL COLORING EXAMPLES

Color in the following.

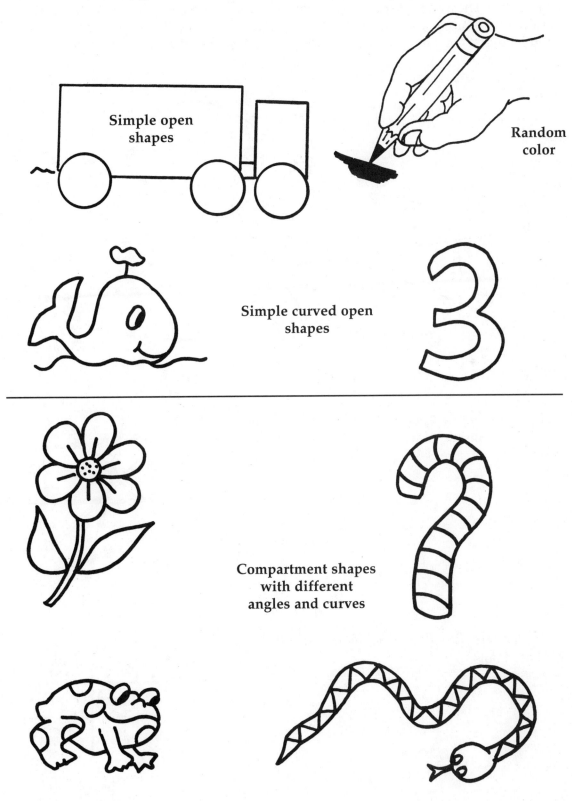

Simple open shapes

Random color

Simple curved open shapes

Compartment shapes with different angles and curves

COLORING GAMES

Coloring games are a stimulating way of introducing pencil control and spatial aspects to children. For young children, explanation of the concepts of the game must be clear and is best shown by example. You may want to start off with larger areas first, then gradually reduce the size of the compartments to be colored. For the games illustrated here, the first child to color the last compartment is the winner.

1. *Color It In.*

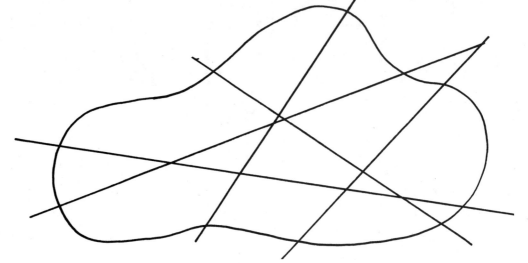

2. *Coloring Chopsticks.* This is excellent for visual discrimination as well as pencil control.

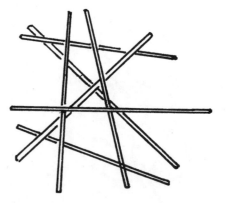

3. Play *Tic-Tac-Toe* using colors instead of symbols.

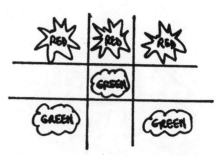

CHANNELING

Channeling is drawing a line between two guiding lines and is the prerequisite to tracing skills. The two lines provide the spatial restraints to which the child must conform. Channeling requires the child to demonstrate visual tracking as well as pencil-control skills while the channel provides for a margin of error.

When providing these activities to children, insist that they try to complete the channeling without changing the position of the paper. This can be achieved initially by taping the channeling task onto the desk. This makes the child complete all the shapes in the required manner. For example, if a child has difficulty moving around a curve, he or she may continually move the paper so that he or she completes the curve as a series of small straight segments. The child must also be encouraged not to change hand position to accommodate directional changes in the channeling activity.

Progressive samples of different shapes to trace are illustrated on the following pages.

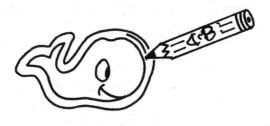

TIPS:

➤ Before having children commence these channeling activities, have them complete tracings around and inside templates. These are good developmental activities that provide physical as well as visual guidance to the movement. Start with the template taped to the paper so the child can concentrate on the pencil control, not stopping the template from moving.

➤ You may want to use finger painting for initial channeling activities. Start with simple activities and move to more complex channeling exercises; for example, between straight wide lines and then introducing curves, squiggles, mazes, and the like.

➤ Gradually narrow the width between the channeling lines.

➤ Ensure correct postural and grip technique.

CHANNELING ACTIVITIES

For young children establish an entry point and a finishing point for these channeling activities. Reproduce "Follow That Line" on the next page for each child. It is a sequential example of a simple channeling activity where picture icons have been used as the entry and finishing points. In the bottom picture a dot is used as the starting position and an arrow is used to indicate direction.

MAZES ARE AMAZING!

Mazes provide a challenging means of promoting channeling skills. Children should initially be introduced to mazes that are generous in width, incorporate straight lines, and are not too visually demanding. As both pencil control and visual skills improve, so the mazes can become more complex. The following are some simple maze ideas that can be easily reproduced or you may wish to purchase a commercial product available through educational resource suppliers.

Blackline masters are excellent resources because you can photocopy and prepare student workbooks that contain maze activities along with others. Make copies of the reproducibles on the following pages.

1. *Bird Maze.* With their pencils at the start dot, children draw their way to the finish. "Before beginning the activity, show me the start and finish. Good! Now tell me what you think must happen in order to get to the finish." For example, keep pencil drawing *between* the lines, never through a line.

2. *Skier Maze.* With their pencils at the start dot, children find their way to the finish. "Before beginning the activity, show me the start and finish. Good! Now tell me what you think must happen in order to get to the finish." For example, keep pencil drawing *between* the lines, never through a line. Can you find more than one way to do this?"

3. *Dog 'n Bone Maze.* Increasing visual complexity provides more challenge! "Chase has lost his bone. Can you help find it?"

4. *Firefighters' Maze.* Adding curves to the maze increases the demand for pencil control. "Can you help the firefighters find the quickest way to the fire?"

Name _____

FOLLOW THAT LINE

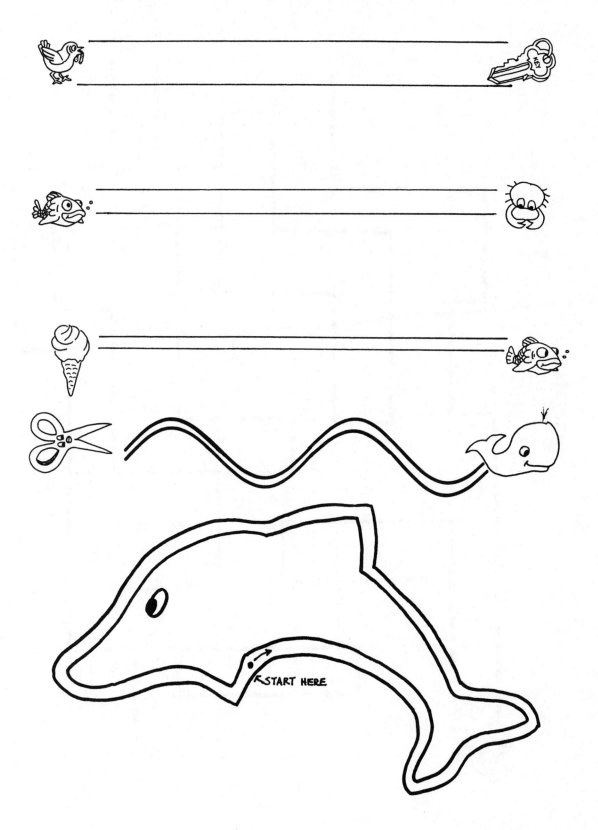

START HERE

Name _____

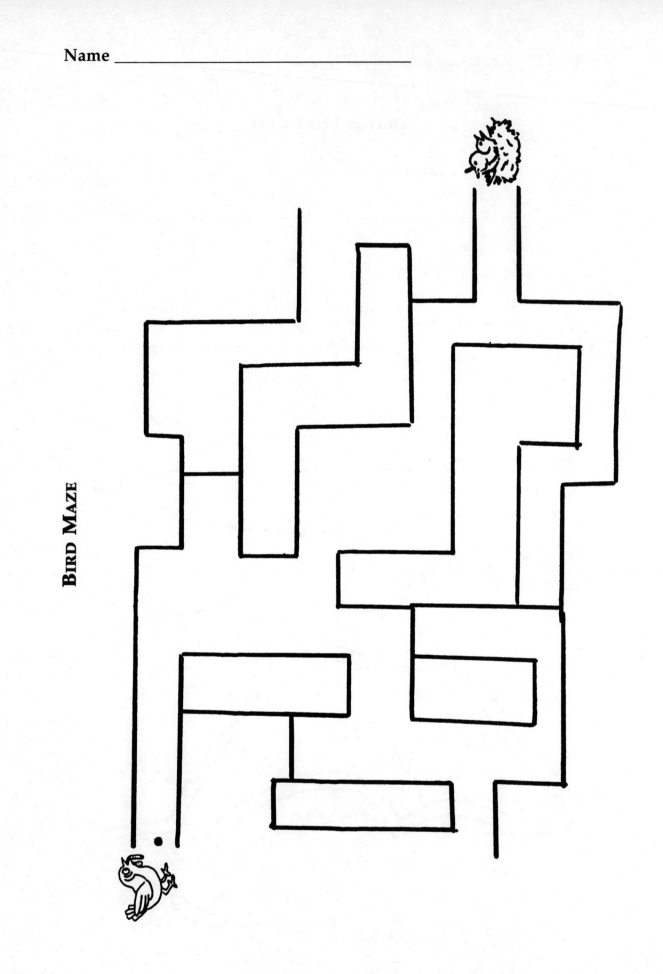

Bird Maze

SKIER MAZE

Dog 'N Bone Maze

Name _____

FIREFIGHTERS' MAZE

Forest Fire!

CHANNELING GAME: GRAND PRIX CIRCUIT

This is perhaps the most enjoyable channeling activity of all and the easiest to produce. The complexity is easily changed by increasing the number of curves and narrowing the track. The activity can be made more challenging by adding race timing and time penalties for hitting the sides of the track. Reproduce "Grand Prix Circuit" on the following page for each child.

RULES:

1. Begin with your pencil at the start position.
2. Trace the track without taking your pencil off the paper.
3. Time the race. (*Optional*)
4. Score a 3-second penalty each time your pencil touches the track.

VARIATIONS:

1. Challenge a partner.
2. Make your own circuit.

GRAND PRIX CIRCUIT

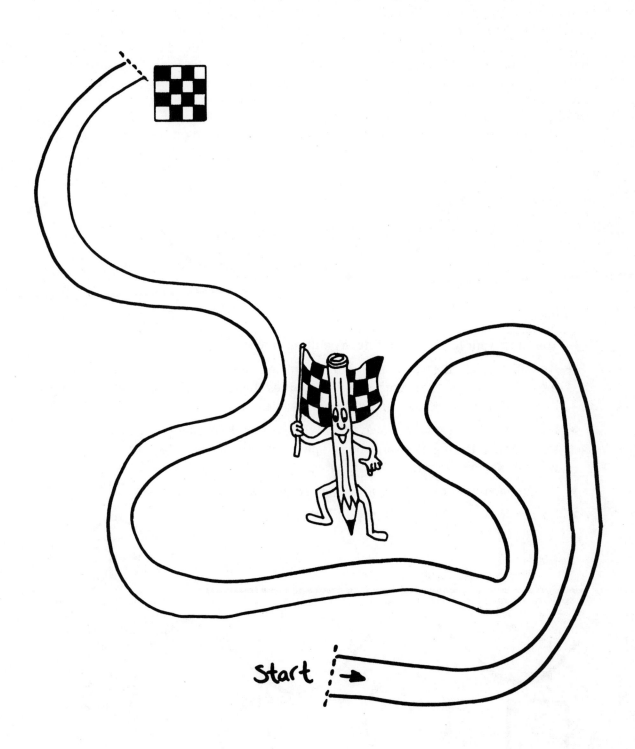

TRACING

The next stage of development is the skill of tracing, which like channeling, requires visual tracking as well as pencil-control skills. When providing tracing activities for children, insist that they try to complete the trace without changing the position of the paper. You can achieve this by taping the tracing onto the child's desk. Children who have difficulty moving around a curve will continually move the paper so that they complete the curve as a series of small straight segments; taping the paper to the desk prevents this. As with channeling, children must be encouraged not to change their hand position to accommodate directional changes in the tracing.

Progressive samples of different shapes to trace are given on the following pages.

TIPS:

➤ You may want to start with finger painting tracing activities.

➤ As with all activities, start with simple tracings and move to more complex tracings. For example, start with simple activities that promote tracing along straight lines and then introduce curves, squiggles, etc.

➤ Have child follow the arrows. Start with a solid line, then dots relatively close together. As tracing skill improves, space dots further apart and replace arrows with numbers or letters of the alphabet.

➤ Closure activities can be introduced as an extension of tracing.

➤ Ensure correct postural and grip techniques.

TRACING ACTIVITIES

1. *Follow the Kite.* Make copies of the reproducible on the following page and give these directions to the children. "Trace your pencil along the kite string to find out which kite belongs to each child. Use different colored pencils as indicated."

2. *Target Drawing.* This more advanced tracing activity reinforces proper pencil grip, arm transport, and visual tracking.

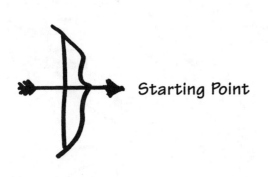 Starting Point

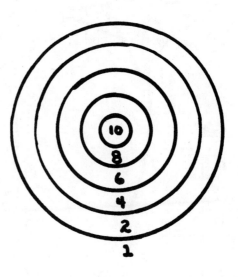

RULES:

1. Place your pencil at the tip of the arrow head.
2. In one *quick continuous action,* trace a line to the target.
3. Score points where you stop on the target.
4. Have three turns and total the score.
5. Play with a partner and use different colors.
6. Make your own target.
7. Increase the challenge of task by increasing the distance.

3. *How Many Putts?* Have child place pencil on golf ball and trace a line to the hole.

Player 1

Player 2

Name _____

FOLLOW THE KITE

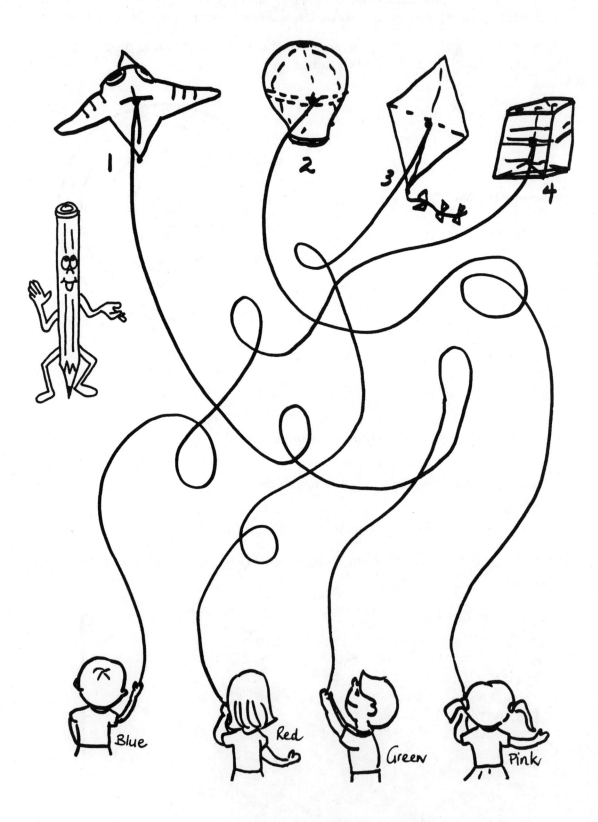

TRACING ACTIVITIES *(Continued)*

4. ***The Dot-to-Dot Chicken.*** Make copies of the reproducible on the following page for the children. "Using your pencil or a colored marker, connect the dots in the direction shown. Then color in your picture."

5. ***Find the Dinosaurs.*** Make copies of the reproducible on page 93. Using numbers and letters adds a sequential cognitive task to the activity.

6. ***Squares.*** Have children find a partner. Each partner has a different colored pencil. Give each pair a dotted sheet of paper as shown on page 94.

The object of the game is to see which partner can make more squares by connecting dots only two at a time, vertically or horizontally. When a player completes a square, he or she colors it in. When there are no more squares to be completed, each player counts up his or her colored squares to see who is the winner. Change partners and play again!

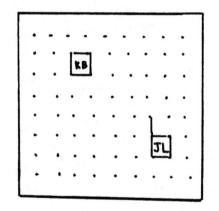

THE DOT-TO-DOT CHICKEN

Name _____   **FIND THE DINOSAURS**

SQUARES

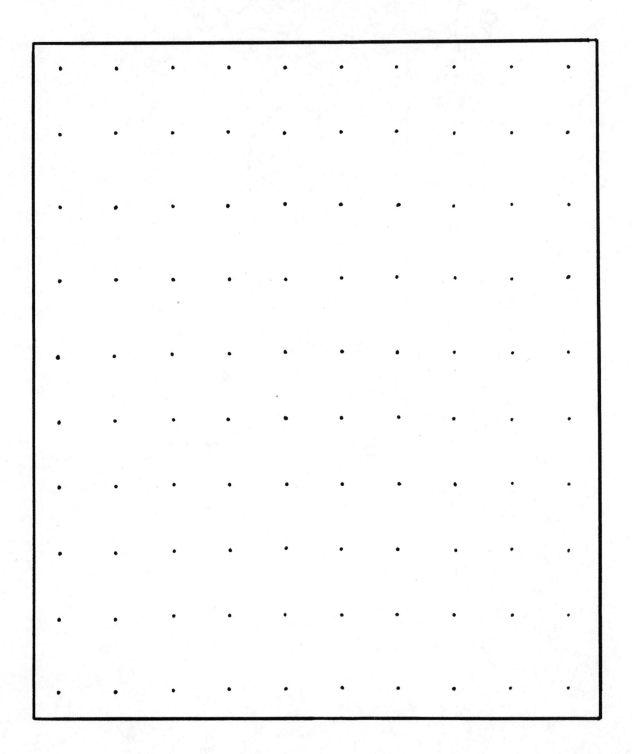

COPYING

Copying involves the skills of pencil control, visual discrimination, and visual motor integration. (See "Tracing.") It is through the ability to copy that children gain the necessary knowledge and skills to acquire formal handwriting and drawing skills. Later in life individuals add their own style and creativity to these skills.

TIPS:

➤ The progression for copying begins with tracing activities with a strong kinesthetic feedback; for example, the child using a finger to trace shapes and letters on varying textures of sandpaper or in sand trays. Once this is mastered, the child moves onto the task of copying on paper using the following progressions:

 Copying simple lines and shapes

 Copying more complex shapes

 Completion activities

 Reproducing pictures and diagrams of different complexity

➤ If a child is experiencing difficulties with copying, then the following progression should be followed:

 Have the child watch you draw the pattern in parts and then copy these parts accompanied by your verbal instruction and kinesthetic assistance, if necessary.

 Have the child copy the whole pattern after demonstration. Use verbal instruction to assist.

 Have the child copy after your demonstration without verbal assistance.

 Have the child copy without demonstration.

COPYING ACTIVITIES

1. *Copy This.* Make copies of the reproducible on page 97. This activity gives some simple progressions for copying.

2. *Complete the Picture.* Make copies of the reproducible on page 98. "Look at the pictures carefully. Can you see the missing part in each? Fill in the missing parts. Then color in the pictures!"

3. *What's Missing?* Make copies of the reproducible on page 99. "Look at the pictures carefully. Can you see the missing part in each? Fill in the missing parts. Then color in the pictures!"

4. *Something's Missing!* Make copies of the reproducible on page 100. "Look at the pictures carefully. Can you see the missing part in each? Make both pictures the same. Then color in the pictures!"

5. *Samantha and Max.* Make copies of the reproducible on page 101. Now children are ready for more visual challengers! "Look at the pictures carefully. Can you see the missing part in each? Make both pictures the same. Then color in the pictures!"

6. *Make Them the Same.* Make copies of the reproducible on page 102. "Look at the pictures carefully. Can you see the missing part in each? Make both pictures the same. Then color in the pictures!"

7. *Make Up Your Own.* Have each child make up his or her own drawing. Photocopy it, then use the first drawing to trace it beside the photocopied drawing, but with parts missing. Swap with other classmates and challenge children to make the drawings look the same. Or you can make copies of the reproducible on page 103 for children who have difficulties drawing.

Name _____

COPY THIS

COMPLETE THE PICTURE

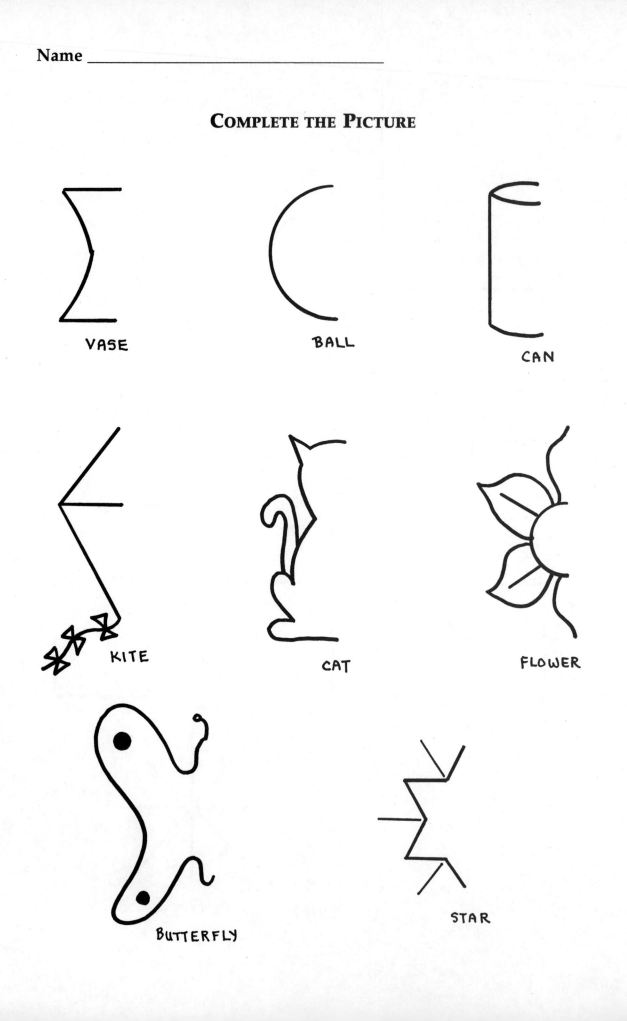

VASE

BALL

CAN

KITE

CAT

FLOWER

BUTTERFLY

STAR

Name _____

What's Missing

UMBRELLA

NUMBER
"EIGHT"

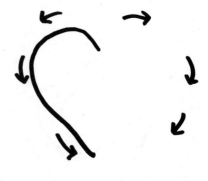

HEART

CUP

EGG

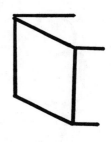

BOX

SCISSORS

POSTMAN

SOMETHING'S MISSING!

Name _____

SAMANTHA AND MAX

Samantha,
the Seahorse

Max, the Basketball Player

Name _____

MAKE THEM THE SAME

MAKE UP YOUR OWN

DRAWING GAMES

1. **Draw the Dog.** Divide the children into groups of 3. Give each group 1 die. Each member of the group has a pencil and paper. Put on whiteboard or a large sheet of paper the following information:

> Each number on the die represents a part of the dog as follows:
>
> 1—eyes and mouth; 2—ears; 3—whiskers; 4—body; 5—head;
> 6—tail and feet.

Children, in turn, throw the die, and draw on his or her paper the part of the dog that the number represents. Who will complete their dog first?

VARIATIONS:

➤ Draw the cat. Draw the mouse. Draw the insect. Let each group decide what body parts the numbers on the die will represent.

➤ Have children work together on one drawing, each contributing in turn, to create the drawing.

2. **The Octopus Game.** Play the game as above to draw the octopus with each number on the die representing the following body parts: 1—1 tentacle (arms); 2—2 tentacles (arms); 3—eyes; 4—head; 5—mouth; 6—baseball cap.

3. Play **Junior Pictionary,** which is commercially available.

FOLDING

Folding is a bi-manual task that initially requires both hands to work simultaneously to achieve the spatial aspects (the fold). The preferred hand completes the creasing action while the non-preferred hand provides stability or guidance to the paper.

FOLDING ACTIVITIES

1. The following are progressive samples of folding activities.

   ➤ Fold the following shapes:
   Square: in half, diagonally
   Rectangle: length in half; width in half
   Circle: in half; in pie shapes

   ➤ Draw lines across a piece of paper and have the children fold along these lines.
   A fan can be made this way. An alternative is to have the children fold the edges of the paper to these lines.

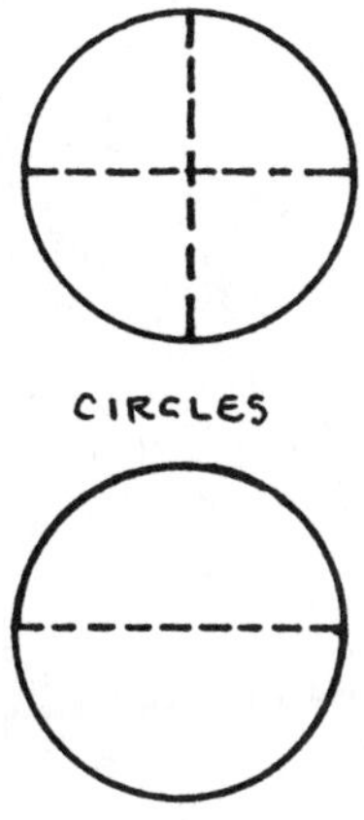

CIRCLES

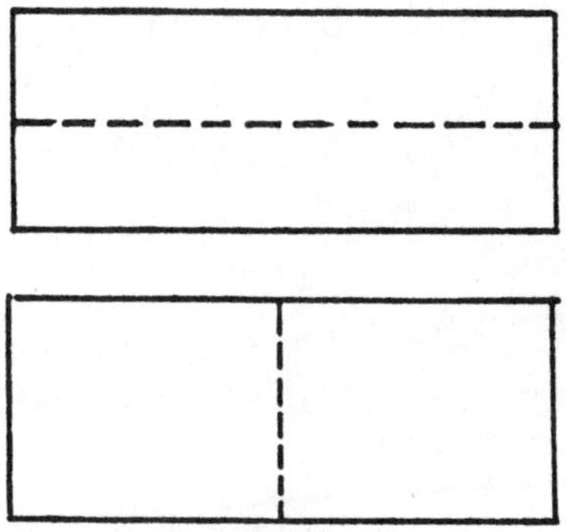

RECTANGLES

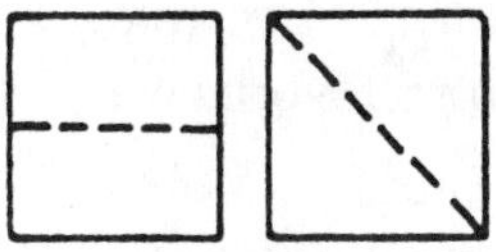

SQUARES

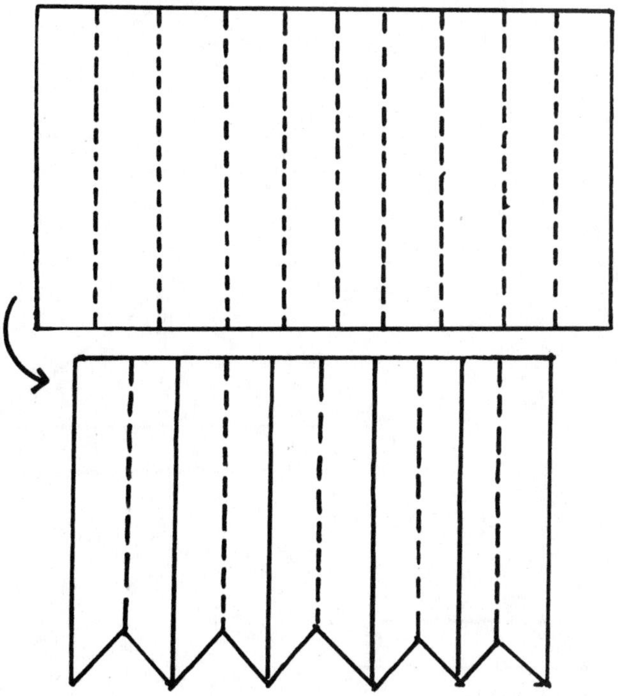

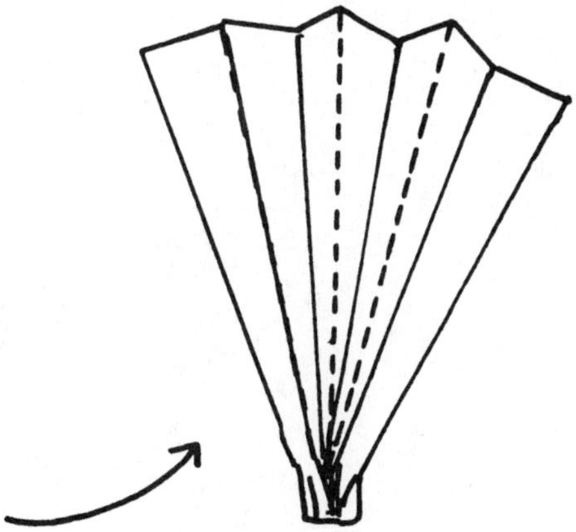

PAPER FAN

FOLDING ACTIVITIES *(Continued)*

Note: Once the children are displaying good coordination in these simple folding tasks, then more difficult and interesting activities can be completed such as those demonstrated below. These activities also develop and enhance listening skills, as well as provide right/left discrimination practice. Origami books are full of ideas for folding.

2. *Pirate's Hat.*

Step 1: Using a full sheet of newspaper, fold top half to bottom half.

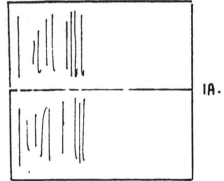

1A.

Step 2: Now fold this in half from left side to right.

Step 3: Open up and fold top left corner to center, then top right corner to center.

Step 4: Fold each bottom strip upwards to complete your pirate's hat.

1B.

Step 5: Decorate and color the pirate's hat in your own favorite way! Wear it with pride.

Variation: In Step 4, fold in the corner strips to create a "sail boat."

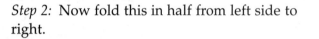

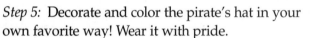

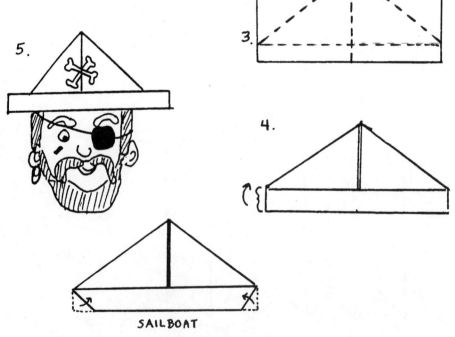

SAILBOAT

FOLDING ACTIVITIES *(Continued)*

3. *Paper Airplane.*

Step 1: Using 8 1/2″ × 11″ paper, fold top half to bottom half, then open up.

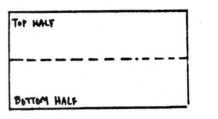

Step 2: Fold bottom left corner to center fold line. Then fold this part to center again.

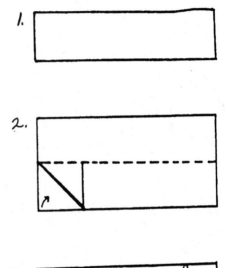

Step 3: Repeat Step 2 with the top left corner.

Step 4: Now fold your paper in half again along the fold line.

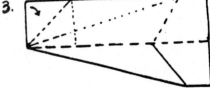

Step 5: Fold each flap top to bottom line. Open as shown. Now your plane is ready. Show me how you can decorate the wings and make it very colorful. Test your paper plane and let it fly! Can you fly at or into a target? Whose plane will fly the farthest?

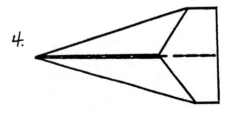

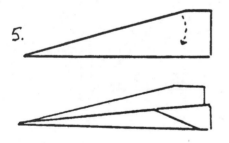

FOLDING ACTIVITIES *(Continued)*

4. *Fortune Cookie.*

Step 1: Fold square in half as shown (bottom to top/left to right).

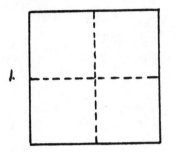

Step 2: Fold each corner of square into center and number as shown.

Step 3: Turn this smaller square over and again fold each corner into the center.

Step 4: Open up each flap and write a "good fortune" message in it. Fold it back to center, then color each triangle a different color.

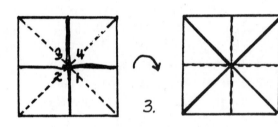

Step 5: Fold bottom half to top half; open up, then fold left side to right side; open up.

Step 6: Slip thumb and pointer finger of each hand underneath flaps to open up your "fortune cookie." Move sections forward or backward. Now you are ready to use your fortune cookie and tell someone his or her fortune.

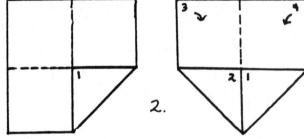

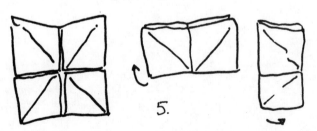

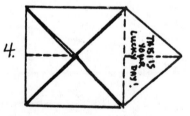

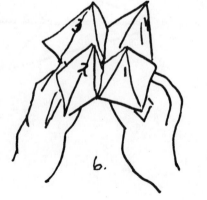

TEARING

TEARING ACTIVITIES

The following are progressive samples of tearing activities. Use these and then develop your own to give to the children.

1. Tear around the dotted perimeter and then around the shape.

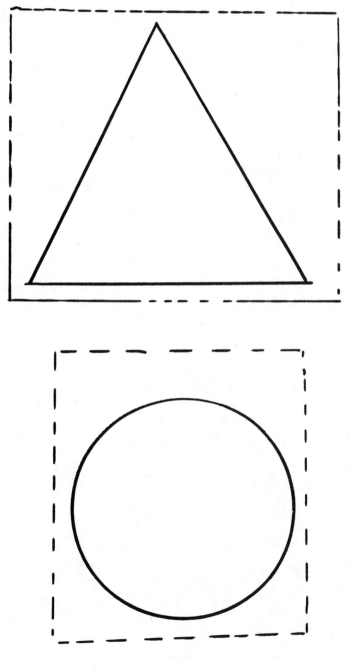

TEARING ACTIVITIES *(Continued)*

2. ***Percy, the Pig.*** Tear magazine pages into small shapes and paste inside the shape of Percy, the Pig.

3. ***Paper Jigsaw.*** Partners, each with a magazine page, tear her or his page into about 6–8 strips. Then each partner mixes up the strips and passes them to the other partner. Who can put the page back together again quicker?

TEARING ACTIVITIES *(Continued)*

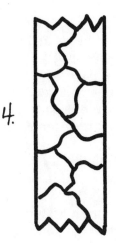

4. ***Bookmark.*** Each child has a piece of cardboard 25 cm × 5 cm (10″ × 2″), 2–3 colorful magazine pages, glue, and a black marking pen. Children tear magazine pages into small shapes and glue onto their piece of cardboard. When the glue has dried, use the black marker to trace (outline) the shapes to create a very interesting bookmark!

   Variation: Use scissors to cut the one end (or even both ends) into a pattern to further enhance the looks of the bookmark!

5. ***Collage.*** With a partner make a collage by gluing onto a large piece of stiff paper:

   ➤ colored paper torn into small pieces

   ➤ crumpled up paper

   ➤ string cut into pieces

   ➤ straws cut into pieces

   ➤ material cut into pieces

   Together give your picture a "title."

6. ***Snake Charmer.*** Each child has several sheets of newspaper or used computer paper, and a leg from panty hose. Tear off some of the paper and crumble up into tight balls. Fill up panty hose leg with the paper balls and tie off the end with an elastic band or string. Use a colored marking pen to make a "face" and "body markings" on the snake. Now pretend that you are a snake charmer and make your snake move!

CUTTING

Cutting is a bi-manual activity that requires the preferred hand to complete an opposition movement between the thumb and middle finger while the non-preferred hand moves the paper and directs it along the correct path. This is a complicated skill for many young children because of the amount of movements that have to be mastered.

The child must (1) control the amount of force precisely so that the scissors' movements are not too large, (2) maintain the correct postural and spatial position of the scissors to avoid twisting actions when cutting, (3) display accurate visual motor and kinesthetic abilities to stay on the cutting lines, and (4) coordinate these actions between the two hands.

An effective way to teach young children to master this skill is to start them cutting out simple shapes between channel lines, beginning with wide channels, then gradually progressing to cutting along single lines. Remember, move from simple to more complex shapes.

TIPS:

> ➤ Cut in small movements depending on shape.
> ➤ Control force.
> ➤ Use the appropriate scissors for right or left handers.
> ➤ Move the paper—not the scissors—when cutting.
> ➤ Cut into plasticine initially, then paper.

SIMPLE CUTTING ACTIVITIES

1. This is an example of a simple channeling cutting activity.

2. *Cut Along the Lines.* Make copies of the reproducible and have children cut along the lines.

MORE COMPLEX CUTTING ACTIVITIES

1. *Straight Lines.*

2. *Diagonals.*

3. *Curves.*

4. *Zigzags.*

5. *Shapes.*

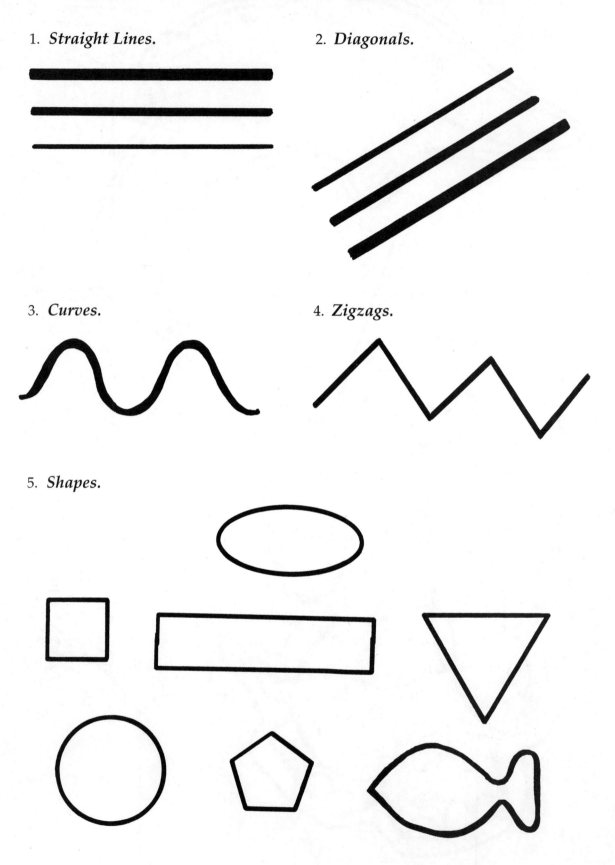

MORE COMPLEX CUTTING ACTIVITIES *(Continued)*

6. *Spirals.* By cutting carefully, cut into one continuous strip of paper.

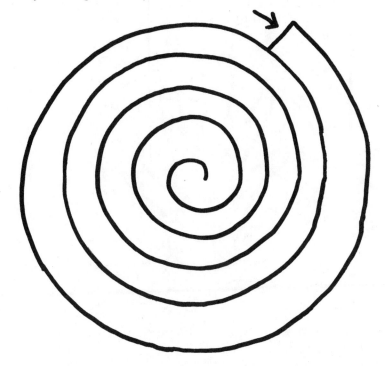

7. *Jigsaw.* Each child selects an appropriate picture from a magazine that he or she can create into a jigsaw puzzle. Then, using black marking pens, draw jigsaw shapes on the magazine picture, glue picture onto cardboard, and let dry. Now cut out the shapes to create a jigsaw puzzle. Mix up the pieces and try to put the picture together again. Swap with classmates and do each other's puzzles!

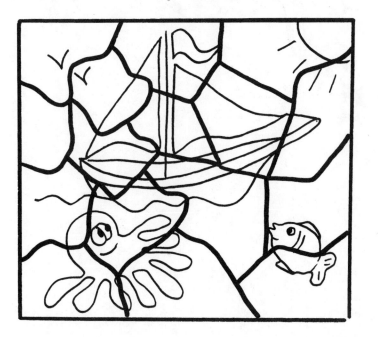

ADVANCED CUTTING ACTIVITIES

1. Have the children trace their own hand. Draw in your fingernails. Name their fingers. Draw a ring on their "ring" finger. Cut out the hand. Ask them, "Can you trace your other hand and cut it out?"

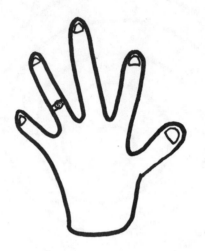

2. *Cut It Out!* Make copies of the reproducible on the following page and have children cut out the shapes.

CUTTING AND PASTING ACTIVITIES

Cutting-and-pasting activities provide an excellent opportunity to introduce concepts such as matching and placement. Use the reproducibles on the following pages.

1. ***Put It in Its Place.*** Make copies of the reproducible. Look at the four boxed pictures to the left. Cut them out and put them where they belong on the chart.

2. ***Half a Face.*** Make copies of the reproducible. "Look at all the half-a-faces! Cut them out and match the halves together to form a whole face. Paste them on a sheet of paper and then color.

3. ***The Bear Family.*** Make copies of the reproducible. "Meet Bert, Betty, and Billy—the Happy-Go-Lucky Bear Family! Color them in, then carefully cut them out."

4. ***The Bear Family Goes Shopping.*** Make copies of the reproducible. "The Happy-Go-Lucky Bear family is going shopping. Help the family get dressed. First, color in their clothes, then cut them out and glue the clothes on the Bear family. Can you figure out which clothes will go on which bear?"

5. ***Clancy the Clown.*** Make copies of the reproducible. "Look at Clancy the Clown on the right side of this page. On the left side are all the clown parts that make up Clancy. Color them in, then cut them out and paste on another piece of paper to look like Clancy."

   Challenge: Have children "create a creature" with detachable parts that can be put together again.

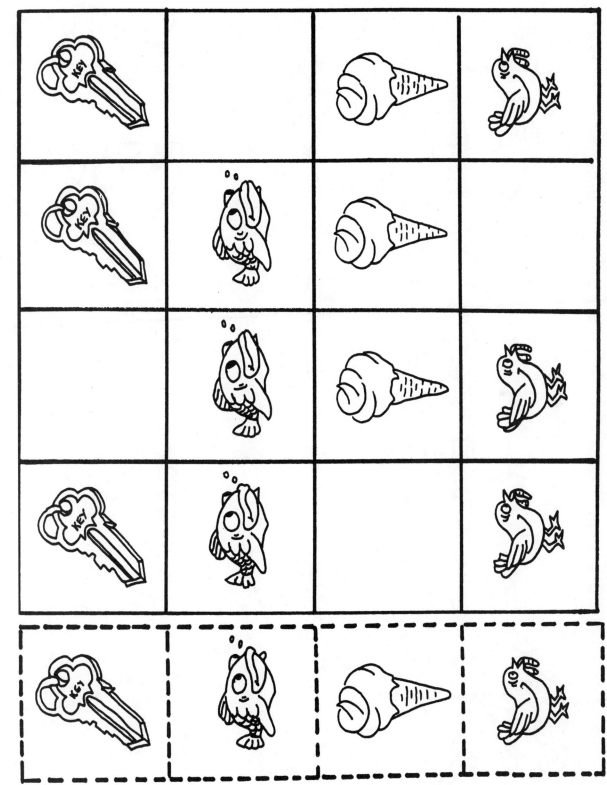

HALF A FACE

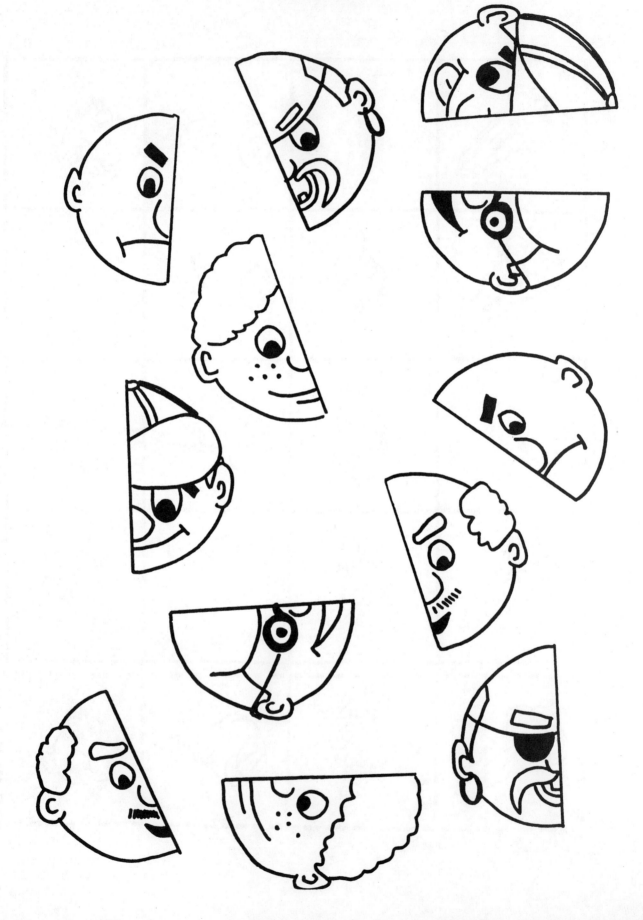

THE BEAR FAMILY

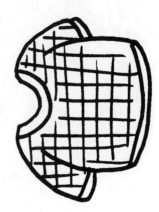

THE BEAR FAMILY GOES SHOPPING

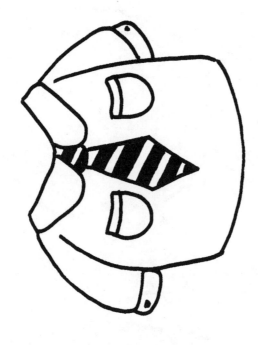

CLANCY THE CLOWN

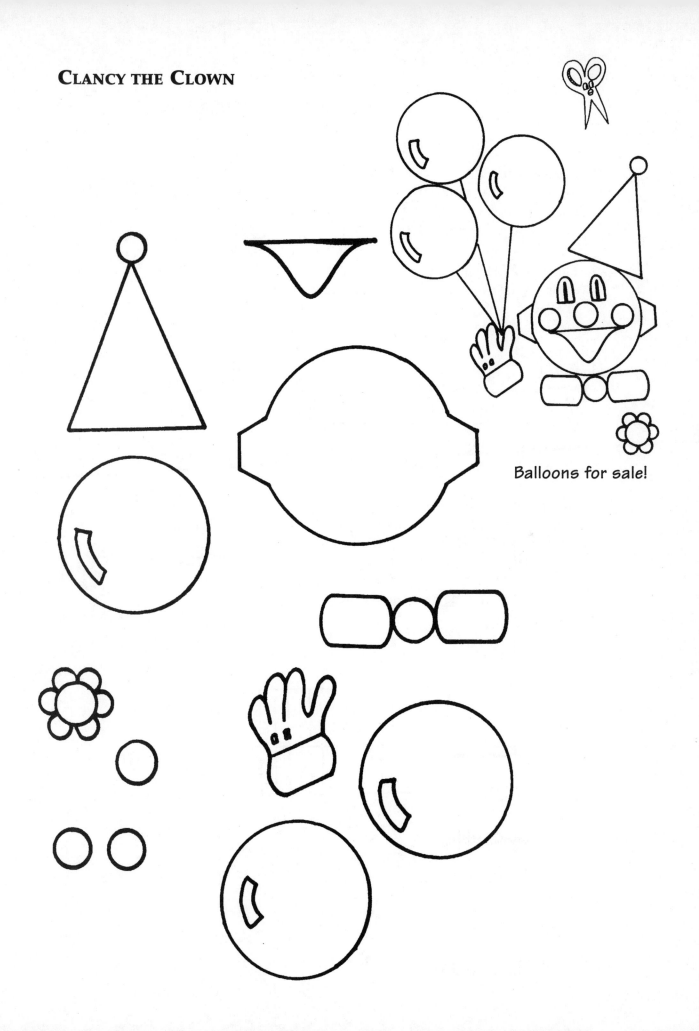

Balloons for sale!

CRAFTY CUTTING ACTIVITIES

1. *My Favorite Pet.* You need a quart milk carton and paper cut into strips about 20 cm (8 inches) in length. Use glue to paste strips along carton to create your favorite pet.

2. *The Mask.* Have child draw a mask shape, color and decorate it, then cut it out. Help child to attach a string or elastic piece to the mask so that it can be worn.

3. *Collage.* Use different materials such as straws, scraps of material, bright colored paper, string, tissue paper, and so on. Make a collage by cutting paper into pieces, straws into small bits, material into different shapes, string into small pieces, crumpled tissue paper, etc.

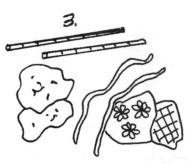

4. *Party Hat.* Each child needs a patterned sheet of paper 20 cm × 15 cm (8″ × 6″), a pencil, and scissors. Cut along the center line, then fold in half and cut along all the other lines, as shown. Open up and gently place your party hat on paper. You may wish to decorate your hat first!

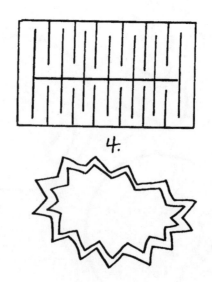

CRAFTY CUTTING ACTIVITIES *(Continued)*

5. ***Egg Carton Snake.*** Each child will need an egg carton, matchbox lid, yarn, darning needle, paint, scissors, glue, marking pens, and piece of cardboard or stiff paper. Separate the egg carton sections by cutting them apart. Then paint sections in different colors or decorate them with marking pens. Paint the matchbox lid and draw eyes on it. Cut out a snake tongue from the cardboard and glue to inside of the matchbox with the forked part protruding. Join all the carton sections together using yarn and needle. Glue yarn to inside of matchbox lid, then extend yarn so that the snake can be pulled along.

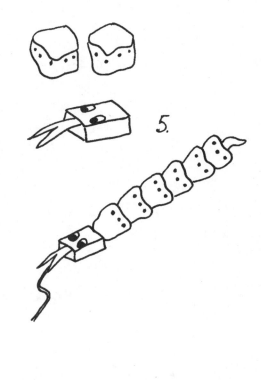

6. ***Accordion Picture.*** Each child will need two magazine pictures (one of a favorite musician, T.V., or film star; the other a land- or seascape), a ruler, glue, and paper (such as used computer paper). For each page, use ruler to draw equal strips down the paper, then cut them out. Now neatly glue alternate strips onto a blank piece of paper. Fold accordion style (one strip one way, the next strip the opposite way). Look at your picture to see the "star" in one direction, and the scene in the other!

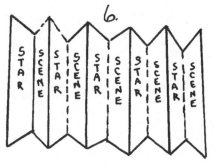

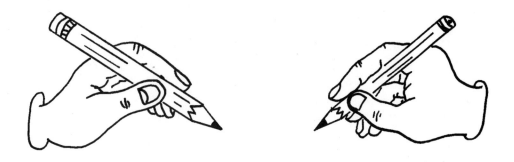

SECTION 5

HANDWRITING

HANDWRITING

Word processing has created a commonly used alternative method of graphic communication to handwriting; however, in schools and especially in the early years, handwriting still remains the main method by which children communicate their thoughts and ideas. Historically, teachers have been encouraged to teach handwriting models and children have adapted as best they can to the model. Realistically we should be attempting to adapt the model to fit the child's needs and physical abilities.

The *method* of teaching handwriting is therefore far more important than the model itself and teaching handwriting should reflect this. The old saying "you can please all of the people some of the time and some of the people all of the time" is no truer than when teaching children handwriting. Handwriting is as individual as the child. All the elements of a particular model are not going to suit all children. Variations exist in adult handwriting, so why not with children's handwriting? After all, a letter is just a visible trace of a hand movement and we all move in different ways, especially in the quality of our movements.

YOURS   MINE

Rigid structure in handwriting can destroy creativity. Alternatively, no structure can often result in the development and automation of incorrect movements that will eventually limit performance and become increasingly difficult to rectify. As in most aspects of life, there needs to be a balance.

A model that teaches the essential movements of handwriting is still an important tool for developing a child's handwriting, but it must only be used as a means to an end; not be the end itself. Flexibility that accounts for individual requirements should therefore become the key component of any writing program.

The emphasis on the goals of handwriting should be to produce a serviceable and versatile style, that can be legible when others are required to read it, and eventually quick enough to cope with the demands of exams and notetaking. Adults, too, must realize that it is not necessary to write neatly all the time and place pressure on children to do so. If this is the case, some children can become consumed with neatness at the expense of fluency and speed. Eventually this will be to the detriment of the child. Neatness still provides the benchmark for what is acceptable handwriting and for beginning writers it is essential to emphasize and teach correct movement characteristics.

The term *neatness*, however, needs to be reevaluated when providing feedback to children. For many children, neatness often means reproducing letters that replicate the model. This is a restriction that is not desirable. Neatness has also the connotation of acceptance or nonacceptance. Children who are struggling with handwriting for any reason—other than a poor attitude—may view this nonacceptance as unsupportive, which can have damaging consequences.

Neatness is a generic term that explains very little. As teachers of handwriting for young children, we need to be more specific. Rather than say to a child "That's not very neat," it is more constructive to say, "I like the way you make the letter 'k,' but I can see you are having trouble staying on the line." After the child has responded, inform the child, "I know how to help you to stay on the line but we are going to have to work on it." Later, once the child is accepting change, you may ask, "Are there any other things you would like to change?" This has multiple benefits. First, and most important, it places the responsibility back onto the child. Second, it gives a chance to provide *specific feedback* on an issue that may be causing the child some concern. Finally, the child will perceive adult support, thus resulting in a safer working environment.

To take responsibility, the child needs to be clear on the requirements of acceptable handwriting; for example, concepts of space, size, and slope consistency, and the characteristics of letter formation.

As children develop writing skills, they must be aware that there are different writing requirements depending upon whether the end product is for their own use or for others to read. For example, in exams there must be a balance between speed and legibility, with the emphasis being on speed. Marks are not allocated for ideas that are still in a child's head!

Research tells us that there are a significant number of students in their final years of schooling who are not finishing written exams or are in considerable discomfort while writing. This is unfortunate because an exam can be difficult and demanding enough, without the additional pressure of inadequate writing speed or physical discomfort. *The roots of these problems lie with the development of incorrect movements from the time the young child begins to experiment with script.*

Once a child starts to show an interest in using letters—for example, writing their name—then this is the time to commence instruction on aspects such as grip, direction, letter formation, and space, albeit in an informal way. *It is of the utmost importance to "get it right" from the beginning!*

This section has been developed to give an insight into the requirements for successful handwriting. Included are examples of the exercises that are useful for this development and strategies to assist those children who find handwriting difficult.

LETTER WRITING

TAKING MESSAGES

FACTORS AFFECTING HANDWRITING

As you can see from the model below, there are many factors that affect handwriting. Let's briefly discuss these aspects.

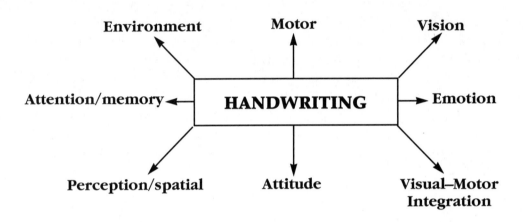

> *Environment:* Environment can affect children in a number of ways. Lack of opportunity to play and experiment with graphic materials will have developmental consequences. Pressure from parents and teachers to perform can cause undue tension. Other factors include inadequate light and poor position of the lighting, the type of writing surfaces (too many things on the desk), and the position of the writer to other people (too close together).

➤ *Motor:* Fine-motor control is an essential foundation for writing skills. Without it the accuracy necessary to guide the pencil through the required formations will be severely affected. Motor planning is required so that the child can accurately reproduce the required shapes.

➤ *Vision:* Difficulties with vision will affect the child's hand–eye coordination which is required for aspects of spatial and motor control. Poor vision is often the cause of many learning difficulties, so adults should be sensitive to emerging patterns.

➤ *Perception/Spatial:* Handwriting has many spatial requirements such as direction, size, shape, slope, and positioning. Spatial problems can make it very difficult for children to create a legible print. *Visual discrimination* is required to distinguish between similar and mirror letters. *Auditory discrimination* is necessary to associate verbal information with graphic forms.

➤ **Attitude:** A poor attitude and an inability to care or take responsibility for one's own actions is arguably the main reason for children's poor handwriting. Children must be trained to take responsibility—and parents and teachers must expect it. Self helplessness is a behavior some children develop in handwriting and in other areas if they are not encouraged to become responsible for themselves. Boys seem to be the main culprits.

➤ **Visual-Motor Integration:** This refers to the child's ability to accurately reproduce shapes. It is the process that links what the eye sees to what the hand produces. Without adequate development in this area, the child is going to have difficulty reproducing the complexities of letter formations and their spatial requirements.

➤ **Attention/Memory:** Without attention to a task, a child will remember little, if anything, and any attempts to learn are futile. It is known that young children respond best to new and colorful stimuli. Because of their short attention span, it is important that our attempts to teach children handwriting are interesting and sessions are shorter.

➤ *Emotion:* Our emotional state can affect our handwriting dramatically. For example, if a child feels uptight and under pressure, it is reflected in his or her handwriting. We cannot expect children to be robots and produce the same quality of written work every day. As their emotional state fluctuates, so may their handwriting.

A Note About Failure

Children learn through want or fear, and the want is created through curiosity and varying amounts of frustration. If the curiosity disappears and frustration or failure becomes too great, then a cyclic process of "writing failure" may result.

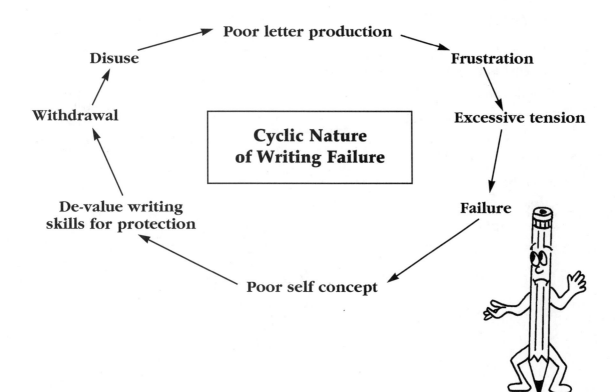

Allow children to work at their developmental level, continually encourage their efforts, and make the sessions as nonthreatening as possible. Keep the activities simple yet challenging and interesting by working in a variety of mediums (visual, auditory, and kinesthetic). Remember to monitor progress, and if the child is struggling, diagnose the difficulty. Adapt strategies to correct these difficulties and continue to monitor the child to assess any changes.

THE WRITING CONTINUUM

As children develop, their motor, perceptual, and cognitive abilities increase. Chronological age is no assurance that a child is ready to commence formal writing, so it is important that children develop sound foundation skills from an early age.

Below is a *suggested* skill continuum for handwriting. Caution, however, must be taken when attempting to define any movement continuum. To place strict timelines on development is like asking how long is a piece of string. All children develop at different rates. Be sensitive to this fact.

3–5 Years

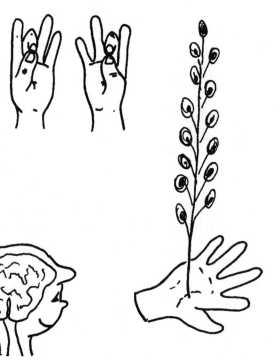

PHYSICAL ASPECTS

➤ Muscle tone
➤ General kinesthetic awareness
➤ Fine-motor control
➤ Correct writing setup

PERCEPTUAL ASPECTS

➤ Body image
➤ Spatial/language concepts related to writing
➤ Visual discrimination
➤ Visual-motor integration

MENTAL ASPECTS

➤ Attention
➤ Memory

5–7 Years

➤ Specific spatial rules
➤ Specific kinesthetics
➤ Consistent language: capital and small letters vs. upper and lower case; capital and non capital; starting stroke vs. entry stroke, joining stroke; exit stroke vs. ending stroke
➤ Formal writing: chronological age is not an indisputable reason for beginning formal handwriting; some children will simply not be ready at 5 years of age, so more time needs to be spent on the developmental skills

- ➤ Patterns
- ➤ Entry and direction of letter strokes
- ➤ Letter rules
- ➤ Family teaching of letters
- ➤ Teach letters with baseline exit strokes first as they promote a more relaxed movement
- ➤ Remediate those children who have experimented with incorrect formations
- ➤ Emphasis is on correct letter formation (neatness)

7–9 Years

- ➤ Teaching running or joined cursive writing when control is apparent
- ➤ Teaching baseline joins, then top joins; reverse joins
- ➤ Encourage children to join letters that they feel comfortable with, not joining all letters

9–11 Years

- ➤ Increasing emphasis on introducing speed with legibility
- ➤ Introduction of speed loops
- ➤ Try different writing implements to foster child's writing skill
- ➤ Automating joined writing

11+ Years

- ➤ More emphasis on speed
- ➤ Notetaking skills
- ➤ Experimenting to find the best way to achieve writing goals

GETTING IT "WRITE"

Handwriting is a hand movement that is guided by the eyes and directed by motor memory.

We have seen handwriting taught by many people, and what appears to be lacking is a systematic, developmental approach that takes into account the many spatial and physical aspects of writing. Remember that children are performing a visual-motor movement, which becomes habitual as they practice. If poor movement patterns are practiced, then these patterns become habitual and difficult to correct.

Give the children precise expectations of what global criteria constitute legible handwriting and ensure that regular feedback in the early stages of handwriting is frequent and specific. When a difficulty or fault in reproduction occurs, do not assume it will correct itself; often it does not.

Instead, supply the child with positive feedback, which will assist the child in correcting his or her script. The correction may be physical, spatial, postural, memory, or simply carelessness, so to say "try again but go slower or be neater," is hardly constructive and of little use to the child unless he or she is obviously rushing the work. It may be more appropriate to have children complete some copying or kinesthetic activities, improve aspects of paper positioning, relax their shoulders, or alter some aspect of their grip.

Do not insist on mirror-image copies. The children must obey certain concepts for legibility, but within these constraints allow for some individuality.

Do allow children to develop at a rate which suits them. Progress through the different aspects of handwriting as the child masters one level allow him or her to move to the next.

WRITING GOALS

As in any movement program, there needs to be goals set that will direct our teaching.

1. Promote correct posture to not only enhance writing skills, but to physically prevent back and visual strain.

WRITING GOALS *(Continued)*

2. Promote effective grip.

3. Ensure all children have the prerequisite perceptual abilities.

4. Promote form and fluency through good developmental teaching and practice.

5. Provide children with the appropriate language skills.

6. Monitor and improve muscle tone so that excessive tension does not occur.

7. Promote correct temporal and spatial combinations of movement among the hand, shoulder, and arm.

8. Develop a positive attitude toward handwriting.

HANDWRITING CHECKLIST

The observation or focus points provided below are followed by a more detailed description of each point. We emphasize the importance of being in the know of what skill(s) are involved in the activity the children are performing and being able to observe for correct technique. Areas of difficulty are also noted.

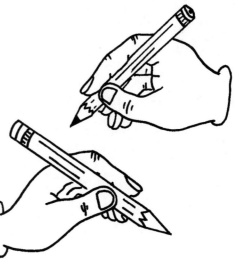

Posture
Muscle tension
Muscle strength
Position of paper
Hand size and shape/grip
Hand-eye coordination
Fluency of arm transport
Force control
Manipulation speed
Hand steadiness
Kinesthetic sensitivity

➤ *Posture:* Correct posture provides the foundation for correct movements.

➤ *Muscle tension:* Correct tension in muscles (not too loose or tight).

➤ *Muscle strength:* Adequate strength in the postural and manipulative muscles.

➤ *Position of paper:* Location of paper for right-handers (tilted left); opposite for left-handers.

HANDWRITING CHECKLIST *(Continued)*

➤ *Hand size and shape/grip:* Correct hand shape and grip for a particular task; perception, estimation, and control of grip size.

➤ *Hand-eye coordination:* Hand–eye coordination is appropriate (accurate hand/finger placement).

➤ *Fluency of arm transport:* Action of the shoulders, arm, wrist, and fingers is fluent. Action of the body movements is in the correct order.

➤ *Force control:* Controlling the amount of force required for manipulation.

➤ *Manipulation speed:* Control of the speed of movement (not too fast or slow).

➤ *Hand steadiness:* Hand movements are steady (reduction of tremors).

➤ *Kinesthetic sensitivity:* The feedback from muscles, joints, skin, and tendons is used to assist in refining movements.

COMMON PHYSICAL PROBLEMS

Children who are experiencing difficulties quite often share one or more common problems. Here are some of these.

➤ Immature or incorrect grip

➤ Too much muscle tension in the grip

➤ Support hand poorly used

➤ Wrist position either too flexed or hyperextended

➤ Posture poor with the back twisted and bent too far forward

➤ Head tilted too much to one side and the eyes too close to the page

➤ Inconsistent spatial rules

➤ Paper is not positioned correctly to the right and tilted left for right-handers; opposite for left-handers

➤ Arm transport is not smooth

➤ Arm position is either too close or far away from the body

➤ Writing from above or below the line; often to do with wrist position

ASSESSMENT OF THE PHYSICAL CHARACTERISTICS OF HANDWRITING

1. Head Position: L—Left;   R—Right;   C—Center;   T—Tilted
2. Eyes: C—Too close;   N—Normal
3. Back Position: S—Straight;   S—Straight;
4. Arm Position: C—Close to the body;   F—Too far forward;   B—Bent and too far away from the body
5. Wrist Position: S—Straight;   S—Straight;
6. Grip Hold: N—Normal;   N—Normal;   F—Flexed position
7. Grip Pressure: T—Tight;   U—Unusual;   L—Held too low;   H—High
8. Arm Transport: S—Smooth;   N—Normal;   L—Loose grip;   P—Painful
9. Paper Position: F—In front of;   J—Jerky and segmented
10. Support Hand: A—Adequate support;   R—Positioned to the right;   L—Positioned to the left;   CT—Paper tilted correctly;   IT—Incorrect Tilt
                                                     P—Poorly positioned;   M—Moves/inconsistent

Name	Head Position	Eyes	Back Position	Arm Position	Wrist Position	Grip Hold	Grip Pressure	Arm Transport	Paper Position	Support Hand

POSTURE

It seems that the way we set up for any movement often determines the success of that movement; such is the case with handwriting. Sound postural foundations can reduce tension and discomfort while placing the limbs in the best position to move freely.

CREATING THE CORRECT PHYSICAL ENVIRONMENT

1. Make sure that when children are writing they have good lighting so that shadows are not cast on the work.

2. Ensure that the desk and chair are the correct height so that the legs are not cramped under desk and the feet are flat on the floor. If this is not possible with the available furniture, then cushions to raise the child can be used and telephone books or something similar can be used on which to place the feet.

3. Clear the writing surface of clutter so that the arms are free to move.

4. A soft surface, such as a book placed under the paper, is easier to write upon.

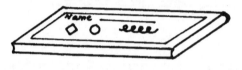

5. Appropriately sized materials, including pencils and paper ends, need to be considered. Pencils that are too thick or thin cause unwanted grip problems while paper size can dramatically affect arm positioning when young children write.

6. A tilted writing surface is of great benefit to some children as it puts the surface of the paper at a friendlier angle to the eyes.

7. In the classroom, check to make sure the child is sitting parallel to the board.

8. In the classroom, do not sit right- and left-handers together if they are sitting in close proximity to each other.

PHYSICAL CHARACTERISTICS OF GOOD POSTURE

1. Relax the neck, shoulders, arms, wrist, hands, and fingers using the exercises described in Section 1, *Body Management*.

2. Sit with the back straight, ideally bending slightly forward from the hips—not the neck.

3. The feet should be flat on the floor.

4. The paper must be positioned correctly in relation to the midline of the body. For right-handers, this means to the right of the midline with the top left-hand corner of the paper tilted downward. The opposite is appropriate for left-handers, with the paper being perhaps a little more tilted.

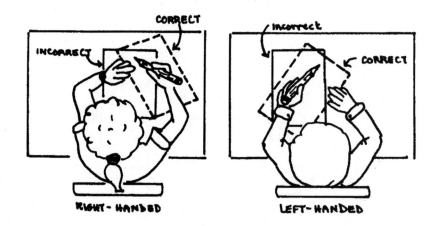

5. The arm should be in a position where it can move freely from the shoulder. You do not want the child to have his or her arm cramped or with the elbow facing away from the writing page. This last position can be derived by sitting on a chair that is too low.

6. The wrist, hand, and finger positions are discussed later on pencil grip.

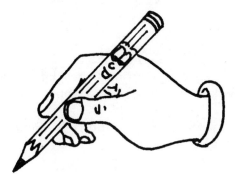

Tip: Excess tension can be relieved by completing relaxing scribbles.

HANDWRITING SPATIAL CONCEPTS

Understanding spatial concepts is essential if a child is to conform to the requirements of handwriting. Size consistency, slope consistency, letter and word spacing, as well as direction of letters are fundamental to legible script.

1. The direction of handwriting for left- and right-handers is from left to right, and from the top of the page downward.

I s u z h a   h   y a

2. Each letter has specific stroke characteristics. The starting and finishing positions must be adhered to as well as the correct form and direction.

m d j k f r t x

3. Letters have a specific height based on whether they are letters with just a body, a head and body, body and tail, or all of these characteristics. This height must be consistent at all times.

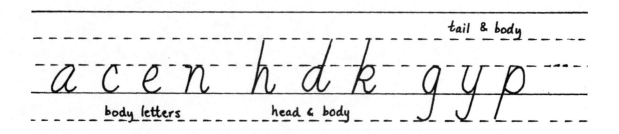

tail & body

a c e n h d k g y p

body letters   head & body

4. Several sets of letters are mirror images of each other, which can cause confusion in young children. As a result, these letters may require more time being spent teaching them.

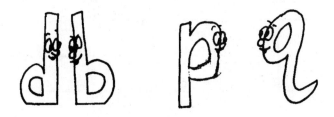

5. Upper- and lower-case letters have specific uses and must be learned by the children.

6. Handwriting requires uniform letter spacing and word spacing.

$fine \ motor$

7. A consistent slope is essential for acceptable handwriting.

8. Most handwriting is completed on lines that provide the upper and lower limits of where letters are placed on the page.

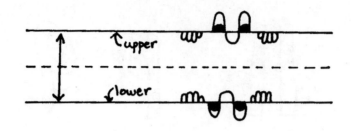

9. Use the reproducible form on the following page to help you assess spatial concepts.

SPATIAL CONCEPTS

Place a C if the concept is consistently achieved.
Place an I if the concept is not achieved consistently.

Name	Letter size C = Consistent I = Inconsistent	Letter slope FC = Forward consistent FI = Forward inconsistent BC = Backward consistent BI = Backward inconsistent	Letter spacing C = Consistent I = Inconsistent	Word spacing C = Consistent I = Inconsistent	Letter direction C = Consistent I = Inconsistent

VISUAL DISCRIMINATION

For children to write successfully, they need to identify the similarities and differences of objects and be able to memorize these. Quite often young children reverse letters; however, it is questionable whether the reversal is due to an inability to discriminate the directional aspects or if the child simply cannot remember the correct directional shape of the letter. A child who is presented identical but mirror-image shapes to compare and cannot distinguish any difference obviously has a discrimination difficulty. A child who writes the letter "b" as "d" could have either a memory or a discrimination difficulty.

Here are some activities you may wish to try with children.

1. Look at the following in each row. Pick out which one is different.

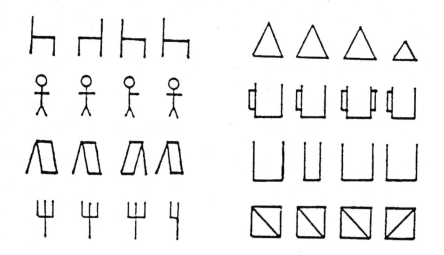

2. Now look at these words. Pick out the one that is the same

an	/	at	an	in	na
no	/	on	in	an	no
mujp	/	jmpu	jump	mujp	mjpu

KINESTHETIC AWARENESS

Kinesthetic sensitivity and memory are important to provide essential positioning feedback which allows us to alter and refine our limb movements. In addition to the exercises described in Section 1, children can be given specific handwriting kinesthetic exercises (movement without the aid of the eyes) similar to the ones described below to enhance sensitivity.

KINESTHETIC ACTIVITIES

1. Use a "feelie" box.

2. Draw lines in different directions. (These need to be copied from a sheet or given as a verbal instruction.)

3. Make similar and different length lines (copied or verbally described to the child).

4. Use lines that have different slopes. (These need to be copied from a sheet.)

5. Draw simple geometric shapes.

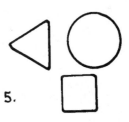

6. Produce letters.

7. Trace letters on the back of the child to see if he or she can identify the letter.

8. *Memory.* Hold the child's hand and trace over different letters and shapes. Ask child to reproduce the trace shape first and then shape size.

9. Trace over or in rough textures surfaces such as on raised letters or in sand.

LANGUAGE ATTENTION AND MEMORY

If a child does not give adequate attention to a task, memorizing that task's requirements—and therefore learning—cannot take place. Promotion of attention is always going to be difficult for those children who lack basic abilities and interest in tasks, so we need to make the sessions as stimulating as possible. Perhaps the first requirement of attention is that the child recognizes, understands, and has an interest in written language and concepts.

When introducing the language and concepts of handwriting, we emphasize the importance of presenting these in a sequential fashion as the child needs them. This gives concepts relevance and will reinforce their meaning. In this way the child can work developmentally on what is appropriate, in a nonthreatening environment. Moreover, language concepts learned here may also be useful for other subject areas such as Mathematics, Art, and English.

LANGUAGE CONCEPTS

Your starting point with the child is to spend some time going through the writing terms. This can be achieved by an adult demonstrating and verbally explaining each of these concepts and then having the child graphically and verbally identify the concepts.

When explaining some language and spatial concepts to the child, you will need a point of reference. This can be easily achieved by using colored lines or an animal or cartoon character as illustrated on the next page. Meet "Tiba," the baby tiger.

LANGUAGE CONCEPTS *(Continued)*

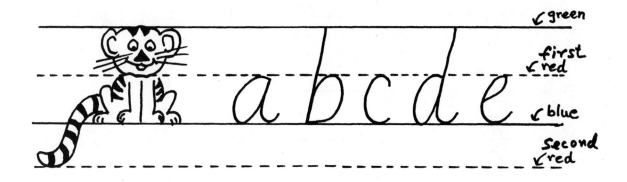

green

first red

blue

second red

➤ *Body:* The part of the letter that starts on the line and goes to the first (red) line or to the tiger's shoulder. Although every letter has a body, there are 13 that only have a body: "a, c, e, i, m, n, o, r, s, u, v, w, x."

➤ *Head:* The part of a letter that goes to the (green) line or to the top of the tiger's head. There are 7 letters that have a head: "b, d, h, k, t, l, f."

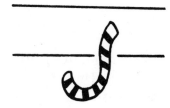

➤ *Tail:* The part of a letter that goes below the (blue) line where the tiger's tail finishes. There are 7 letters with a tail: "g, p, q, y, j, f, z" (in some writing styles).

LANGUAGE CONCEPTS *(Continued)*

➤ *Starting position:*   This is where the letter starts. Every letter has an approximate starting position. The starting position is sometimes an entry stroke.

➤ *Entry stroke:*   Some letters have a small stroke before the body of the letter is commenced: "m, n, r." This stroke is about 45 degrees.

➤ *Ending position:*   This is the point at which the letter stroke finishes. Quite often this is the exit stroke in cursive writing.

➤ *Exit stroke:*   This is a small stroke at the end of a letter's body and is at an angle of about 45 degrees where the letter ends. Most cursive-style letters have these (usually at the tiger's feet).

➤ *Capital letters:*   These are special letters used at special times: start of a sentence, names of people and places. These letters start at the tiger's feet and go up to his head.

LANGUAGE CONCEPTS *(Continued)*

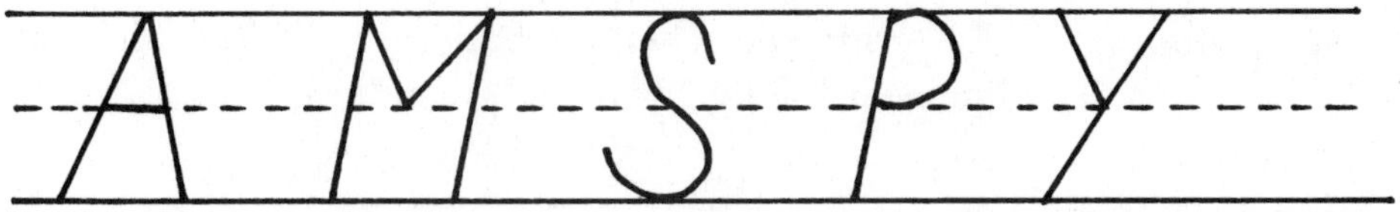

A M S P Y

➤ *Lower case:* This refers to normal writing letters that we use to write most of our words. These letters have combinations of head, body, and tails.

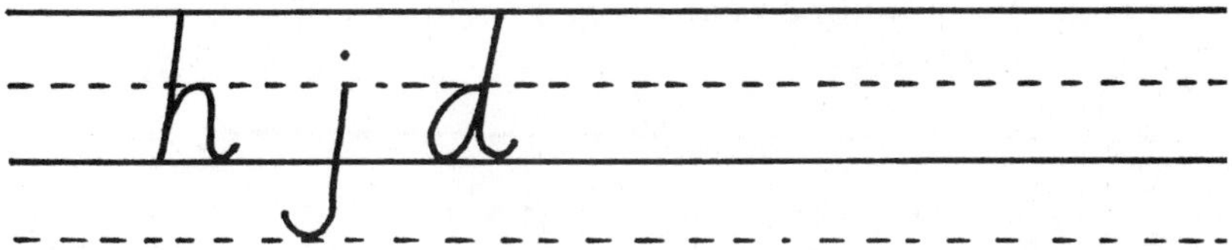

h j d

➤ *Upstroke:* This is a stroke that goes upward. This is the main direction used when joining letters.

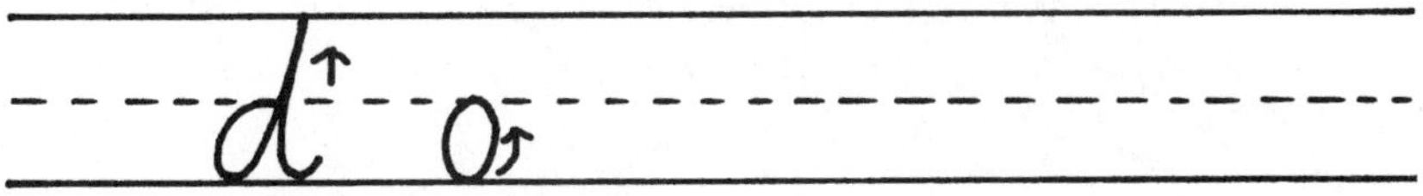

d or

➤ *Downstroke:* This stroke goes downward. This is the main direction used to start letters.

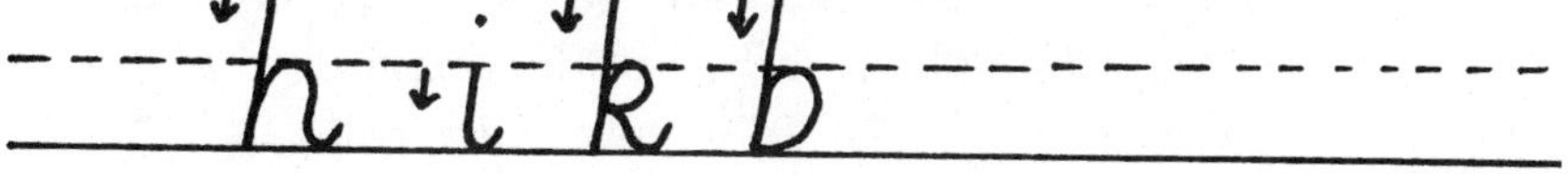

h i k b

➤ *Wedge:* Some writing styles do not retrace when changing directions while forming the letter. Instead, a gap between the upstroke and downstroke is formed.

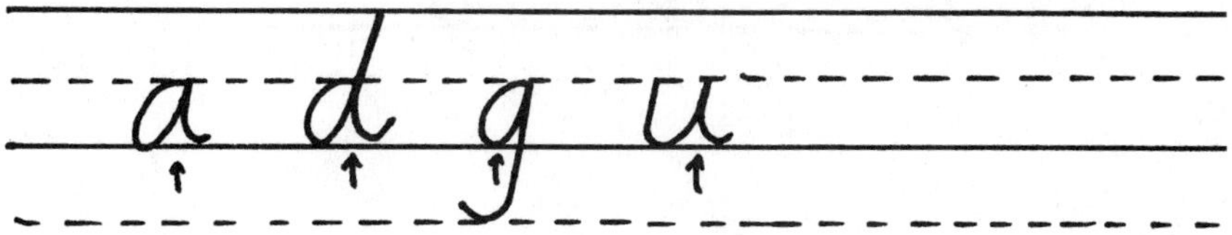

a d g u

LANGUAGE CONCEPTS *(Continued)*

➤ *Above the line:*   The term used when the body of the letter does touch the line near the tiger's head (green line).

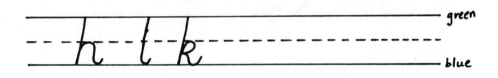

➤ *Below the line:*   The term used when the body of the letter goes below the blue line near the tiger's tail (red line).

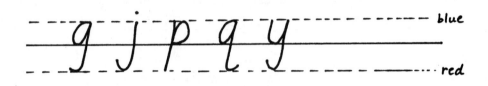

➤ *On the line:*   This is when the body of the letter is between the red and blue lines—the tiger's body.

➤ *Clockwise:*   These are strokes that are curved, oval, or circular. They start at 12 o'clock and go in the direction that the tiger is spinning. (It's like doing a forward roll.)

LANGUAGE CONCEPTS *(Continued)*

➤ *Counterclockwise:* These are strokes that are curved, oval, or circular. They start at 12 o'clock and go in the direction the tiger is spinning. (It's like doing a backward roll.)

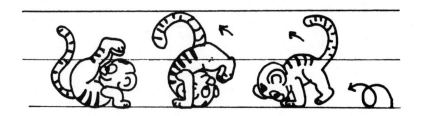

➤ *Vertical:* These lines go straight up and down like a lamppost. In writing they usually start from the top and go downward.

➤ *Horizontal:* These lines start from the left and go to the right. Except for crossing a "t," they are only used in forming capital letters.

E H L T M

LANGUAGE CONCEPTS *(Continued)*

➤ *Crossing:*   In writing this is where two lines that are going in different directions go over each other. Letters that have lines that cross are "f, t, x" and the numbers "4" and "8."

➤ *Dotting:*   Use a dot to put a hat on the letter "i" and to finish all our sentences.

i

➤ Spacing: Use spaces between letters and words so that you can see where one starts and finishes. Spaces between words are about one finger width when you first begin to learn to write.

We   must   have   spaces.

➤ *Slope:*   Writing can lean forward (forward slope), go straight up and down, or lean backward (backward slope). Whichever way you slope your letters when writing, to look good they all must have the same slope.

➤ *Finger names:*   It is important to name your fingers so you can talk about grips.

Index = Pointer   Middle = Tall Man   Thumb = Thumpkin
Fourth = Ring   Fifth = Pinky

LANGUAGE CONCEPTS *(Continued)*

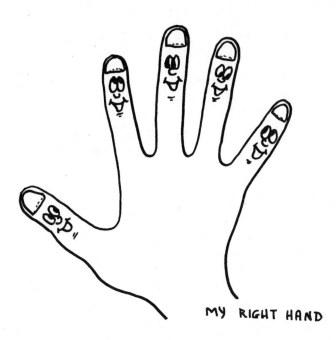

MY RIGHT HAND

➤ *Pressure:*   This is pressing too hard or too soft. You need to get it just right.

Top:

Bottom:

➤ *Joins:*   This is the spot when two letters come together.

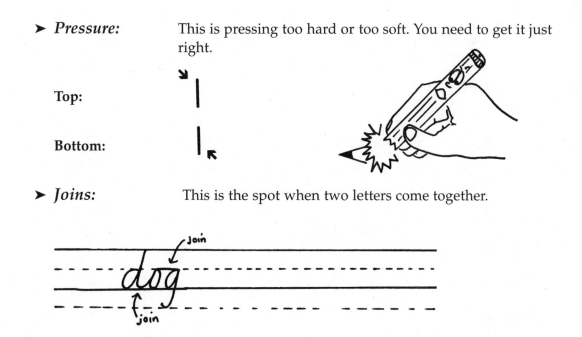

Use the reproducible on the following page to help you assess writing language concepts.

WRITING LANGUAGE CONCEPTS

Place a checkmark in the box when it becomes apparent that the child understands the concepts listed below.

Name	Body	Head	Tail	Starting position	Entry stroke	Ending position	Exit stroke	Capital letter	Lower case	Upstroke	Down stroke	Wedge	Clockwise	Counter-clockwise

Name _____

TIGER'S PRACTICE TIME

b d h k t l f

START HERE!

b

m a c e i m n o r s u v w x

START HERE!

a

g g p q y j

START HERE!

g

AUDITORY MEMORY/LANGUAGE ACTIVITIES

1. ***Tiger's Practice Time.*** Make copies of the reproducible on the following page. "Carefully practice forming the letters."

2. To assess and promote auditory memory and language concepts, ask the child to copy a shape as you verbally describe it. For example, draw a line that starts on the line and slopes to the right.

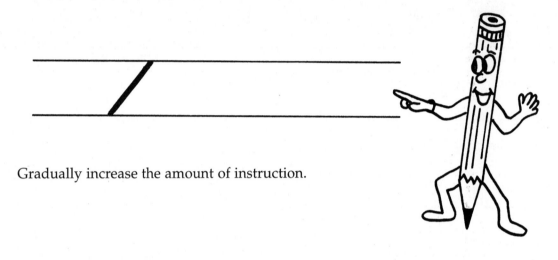

Gradually increase the amount of instruction.

3. Draw a clockwise oval and then draw a line (horizontal) across the top of the oval so that it touches the top of the oval.

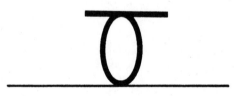

4. Draw a vertical line that starts on the bottom line and then goes to the top. Start at the top of this line and draw another line that slopes to the right, then goes back down to touch the bottom line.

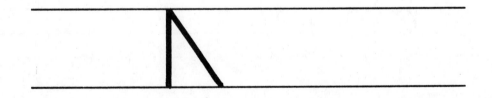

AUDITORY MEMORY/LANGUAGE ACTIVITIES

(Continued)

5. Ask the child to reproduce a letter from your verbal description of the letter; for example, an "h" which has a head and a body. "The head as usual starts with a downstroke. You know where the body starts. The body then curves clockwise to the tiger's feet." Have the child describe a letter for you.

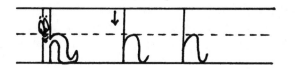

6. ***Story Trace.*** Use different traces to represent movements. Each time the story is told, a locomotor action performed by the character in the story is represented by a trace on the piece of paper. This can be enhanced further by providing a landscape for the children to move through, which then provides spatial constraint for the child to work in and is more demanding. The task is initially performed on a large 18" × 24" piece of paper using fingerpainting, then gradually reduced to 8–1/2" × 11".

Swimming trace

Hopping trace

Walking trace

Running trace

AUDITORY MEMORY/LANGUAGE ACTIVITIES

(Continued)

Story line: Once upon a time **Smiling Dot** went for a walk. Suddenly he fell down a deep hole. Down and down he fell until he reached the bottom. He didn't hurt himself because he had fallen into a giant milkshake. Dot lay on his back and did the backstroke to the side of the milkshake container where there were stairs leading to the top. Dot slowly climbed the stairs. When he reached the top he jumped up and down with joy at the sight of a beautiful valley at the bottom of the hill. Dot was so excited that he didn't see the banana peel—he slipped and rolled all the way to the bottom of the hill!

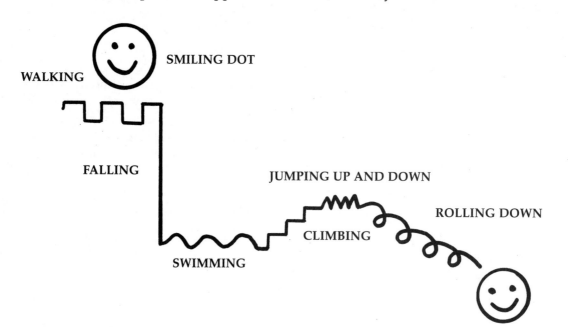

You can now add the spatial constraints by giving the children a landscape in which to place the traces.

MOTOR MEMORY ACTIVITIES

Motor memory is important as it will allow the child to eventually automate the handwriting movements and also allow for feedback to refine movement. Kinesthetic training will enhance motor memory by making the child focus on the movements without the aid of vision. Opportunity to practice is also essential to improve motor memory.

VISUAL MEMORY ACTIVITIES

Visual memory provides the ability to recall letter formations and spatial requirements. This can be enhanced by playing memory games and by having the child complete the following activities.

1. Identify pictures, shapes, and letters that are first displayed to the child and then removed from sight. The child responds verbally. You can extend this activity by giving feedback to the child of those items recalled correctly and then present the items again. Repeat this until all items are recalled or no further progress is being made. Gradually increase the number of items.

2. Have the child copy simple shapes, then letters, that are first displayed to the child and then removed from sight. Follow the same procedure as described in #1.

Tip: Remember to start simply and you will find that attention, memory, and language components can be trained. Weaknesses can be easily seen whereby you can provide enrichment programs. All it takes is some imagination and caring.

COPYING

Once children can discriminate, they then must translate what they see into graphic form. They must have the ability to copy; this is often termed *visual-motor integration*.

COPYING ACTIVITIES

The following is an approximation of what you can expect the child to copy. It is not intended that you use these instructional guidelines for the purpose of assessing the child. If assessment is required, there are specific assessment tools available that can be administered by the appropriate professionals to test the child on spatial and visual-motor integration aspects.

1. *Copying Sequence.* Copying should begin with tracing, initially with a strong kinesthetic feedback; for example, the child uses his or her finger to trace shapes and letters on varying textures of sandpaper or in sand trays. Once this is mastered, the child moves onto the task of copying on paper using the progressions suggested below:

   ➤ Copying simple lines and shapes
   ➤ Copying more complex shapes
   ➤ Copying letters

COPYING ACTIVITIES *(Continued)*

2. ***Teaching Progression.*** The progressions for enhancing visual-motor integration are illustrated here. For each progression, follow this procedure.

> ➤ Child watches you draw the pattern in parts and then copies these parts accompanied by your verbal instruction and kinesthetic assistance, if necessary.

> ➤ Child copies whole pattern after demonstration. Use verbal instruction to assist.

> ➤ Child copies after your demonstration without verbal assistance.

> ➤ Child copies without demonstration.

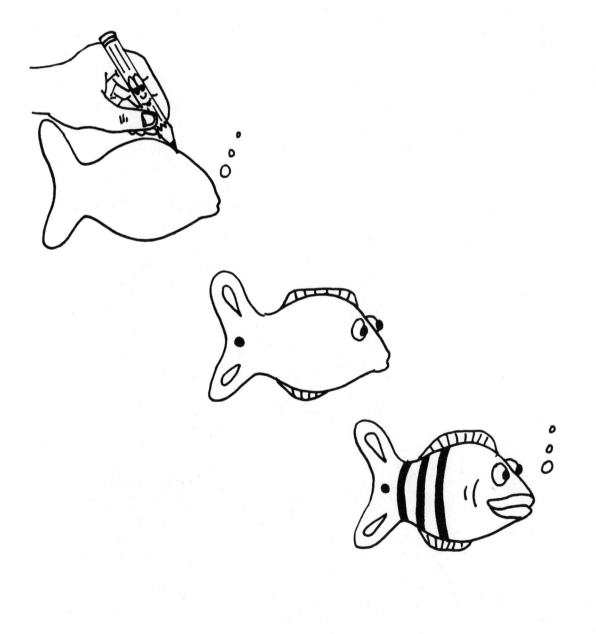

COPYING ACTIVITIES *(Continued)*

3. ***Copying Spatial Aspects.*** Start with copying simple dot diagrams. "Make your drawing look like mine."

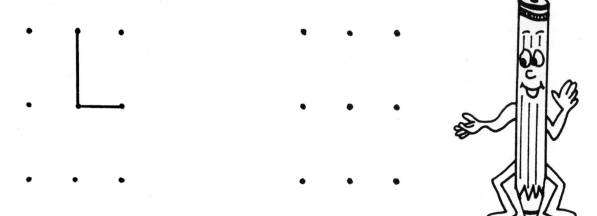

Slowly increase the complexity of these.

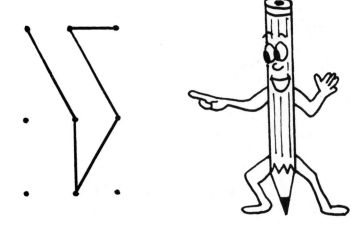

Add more dots and make the diagrams more complex.

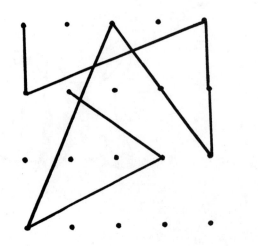

COPYING ACTIVITIES *(Continued)*

Take away some of the dots on the copying page. Start with simple patterns and become more complex.

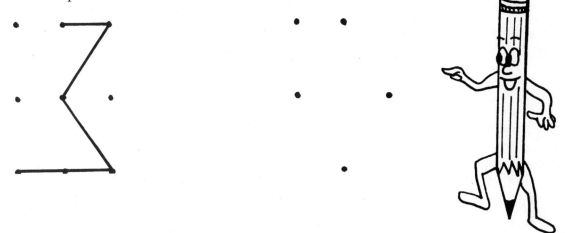

The next stage is to slowly decrease the number of dots on the copying page until the page is blank.

APPROXIMATE AGES FOR COPYING TASKS:

➤ 4 years: 5-dot chart, start at 2, increase to 4 points

➤ 4–5 years: 9-dot chart, start at 4, increase to 7 points

➤ 5–6 years: 25-dot chart, start at 8, increase to 16, and also increase the amount of intersections

➤ 7–8 years: 25-dot chart, gradually decrease the number of dots on copying chart until blank

4. *Copying Simple Shapes.* Have child copy simple shapes. Remember, every child develops at his or her own pace. If you find that the child is having handwriting and copying difficulties—and showing no improvement with practice— then visual problems should be explored and referral to appropriate professionals be taken.

PENCIL GRIP

Some of the more common grips that children might develop are illustrated below, but before rushing off and changing a child's grip, consider this. The grip must:

➤ Allow the child to write legibly.

➤ Write with adequate speed.

➤ Write without discomfort.

If these three concepts are achieved, then the anatomy of the grip is unimportant. Historically, the tripod grip illustrated in Diagram 1, with the pen lying at a shallow angle, originated before the introduction of modern writing implements such as the ballpoint and roller point pens. It has been suggested that with the introduction of these implements, the modern grip is becoming more upright and with less pressure being exerted by the thumb.

Diagram 1

The tripod grip is still the acceptable model, although the unusual grip illustrated in Diagram 2 has been used successfully to release tension and discomfort when writing. Who is to say this is not a more efficient means of holding modern writing tools?

Diagram 2

Whichever grip is preferred by the child, it should allow him or her to achieve writing goals without discomfort. If the child is displaying a grip that promotes tension, restricts movement, causes discomfort, and results in slow writing speed and poor letter formation, then the grip will need to be altered.

Discomfort when writing is associated with improper grips, grip tension, and excessive writing pressure. (Children with long fingers can experience discomfort more often because the fingers are forced to flex more on the pen.)

GRIP BASICS

Although grips vary, the successful grips tend to have some common characteristics. The grip consists of three components, all of which are transported across the page by the forearm:

➤ the fingers

➤ the hand

➤ the wrist

One or all three of these may be the cause of a writing difficulty, so experimentation and careful observation are the key. The following fundamentals have proven to be successful and should be used if the child is experiencing difficulties.

1. The index finger should be at least equal to (Diagram 3) or longer than the thumb (Diagram 4).

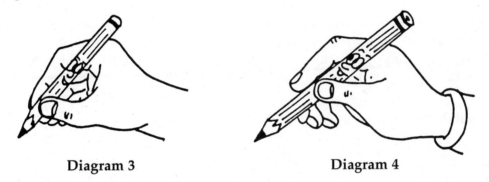

Diagram 3   **Diagram 4**

2. The index finger controls the up-and-down movements of the stroke; the middle finger controls the upward movement; and the thumb bends with each movement and adds stability.

   Tip: If you find it difficult to alter a child's grip, try wrapping some masking tape around the pencil and placing three different colored dots on the tape where the fingers should be placed.

3. The wrist should be relaxed and straight, *not* curved as shown here.

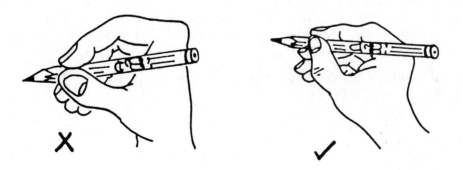

GRIP BASICS *(Continued)*

4. The hand provides support for the fingers and should not be too upright or flat, as this will cause discomfort and slow writing in many cases.

   Tip: A hooked hand causes the hand to be too much on the edge.

5. If the pressure is spread equally in the tripod grip or the thumb applies pressure to the middle finger, the pen tends to lie low in the hand. If the thumb applies pressure to the index finger, the pen is seated higher in the hand. Pulling the index and middle fingers up toward the palm also causes the pen to sit higher in the hand.

   Tip: The left-hander should be encouraged to place equal pressure among the thumb, middle, and index finger to keep the pen low in the hand.

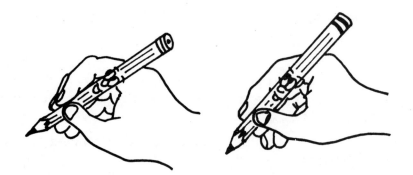

6. The grip for a right-hander should be about 2.5 cm (1 inch) from the tip of the pen. For left-handers, the grip should be approximately 3.5 cm (about 1-1/2 inch) higher. This helps prevent the child from hooking his or her wrist and enables the child to clearly see what he or she is writing without dropping the head to the side.

   Tip: If the child keeps moving the fingers down, place some tape on the pencil so the child can feel the position.

GRIP BASICS *(Continued)*

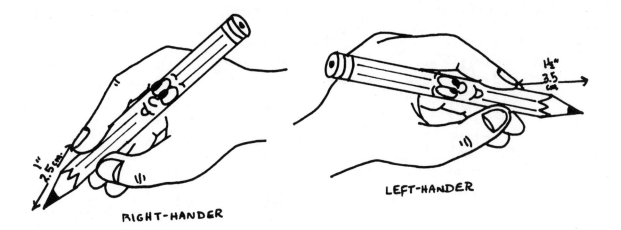

RIGHT-HANDER

LEFT-HANDER

7. Grip pressure should be relaxed. (Look for the dreaded white knuckles.) The fourth and fifth fingers must be relaxed to assist in a fluent movement. If they tighten, the wrist becomes very stiff.

8. The forearm pulls the hand across the paper.

   Tip: Tell the child that you pull the pen across the page like a train pulling carriages.

GRIP BASICS *(Continued)*

9. Writing implements are a matter of choice, but initially for young children a soft point that moves freely over the paper is preferred. Some people say that thicker pencils are best for young children, which is interesting because it has been shown that when left to experiment with different sized pencils, children more frequently chose the normal thickness implement! Common sense tells us to let the child experiment and find what is comfortable.

10. The grip should enable the child to write from the *side* of the line, definitely not from above the line and preferably not from below.

    Tip: Don't get confused. The hand is below the line so that the child can see what is being written, but the point of the pen is entering from the side.

11. The pencil trace should be light to promote directional changes and fluency. If grip tension is excessive, then this is difficult to achieve.

    Tip: If pressing too hard is a problem, then have the child draw on a piece of paper that has carbon paper underneath so that an imprint is achieved on the bottom layer of paper. You draw and compare the darkness of color of the traces. The child can clearly see the difference and can experiment with pressure until the trace lightens to a color similar to yours. You could also ask the child to write on tissue paper without tearing it.

PENCIL CONTROL

Pencil control relies on precise motor coordination. Motor planning is essential for successful handwriting and, therefore, should be developed before formal handwriting begins.

The writing movement must be a combination of finger movements and arm transport. A common fault observed in young children is to use only the fingers to control the pencil. Excessive bending and straightening of the fingers occur with little wrist or arm movement being involved. Before pencil-and-paper tasks are begun, the children should be able to complete the fine-motor tasks presented in Sections 2 and 3.

Below are some of the ways in which pencil control and letter formation can be enhanced. Examples of pre-writing activities that use these same concepts are illustrated in Sections 2 and 3.

Note: Shape reproduction is discussed earlier in this section under the topic Visual-Motor Integration, with the basic progression beginning with tracing, then copying simple shapes, and then moving on to production of letters.

The pencil progressions for letters include:

➤ Patterns
➤ Coloring in
➤ Channeling
➤ Tracing
➤ Fading

Patterns

Coloring in

Channeling

Tracing

Fading

PATTERNS

A child has to master specific patterns to be able to commence writing. These basic shapes are illustrated below and should be practiced in interesting ways.

For all these shapes, they should first be practiced by using large strokes, such as in finger painting, that are freely spaced on the page. The progression is to reduce and vary the size of the strokes as well as the speed they are copied. The final stage is to use lines and boxes as spatial boundaries.

➤ Straight vertical line (practice different sizes and different speeds)

➤ Slanted vertical lines

➤ Counterclockwise circular or oval shape

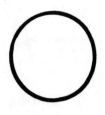

➤ Straight horizontal lines

PATTERNS *(Continued)*

➤ Clockwise curve

➤ Combinations of the above

Here are other patterns that can be practiced with the child.

PATTERNS *(Continued)*

The way you can have children practice these shapes can be as varied as your imagination. Commercial publications use pictures with shape themes, as shown. These are relatively easy to produce yourself and provide a stimulating way to present patterns to young children.

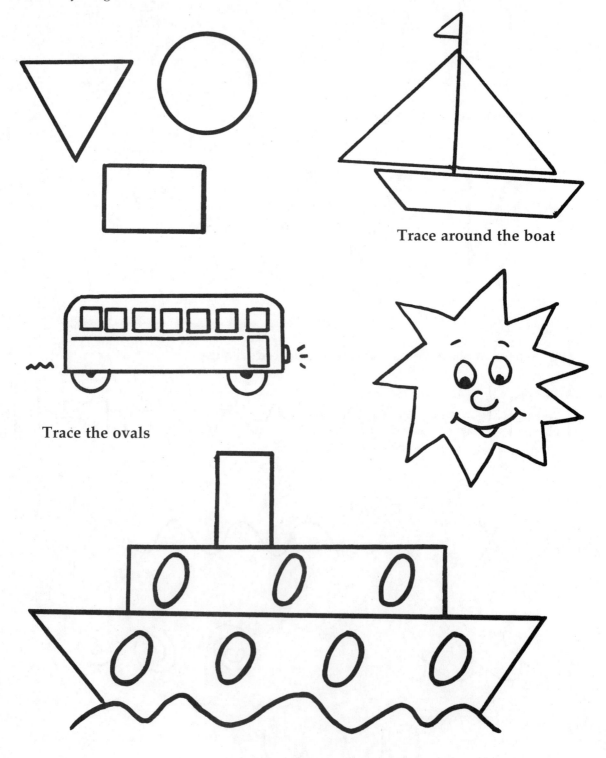

Trace around the boat

Trace the ovals

COLORING IN LETTERS

This can be best achieved with young children by giving the letters some character or animation, as shown. The alphabet is presented in this form in Section 6. The letters should start off large; then, as the child shows efficiency at coloring, the letters can be reduced.

CHANNELING

This is the first activity that introduces the concepts of letter formation and direction. The child is required to start at the marked point (entry stroke) and trace inside the letter as accurately as possible. The letters should start off large; as the child shows efficiency at tracing, the letters can be reduced in size. The channeling alphabet is presented in this form in Section 6. Here are some examples.

    Note: The cursive and manuscript style of letter writing are presented in this book. If education systems use other styles or methods (such as the "ball and stick"), simply *adapt the concept of channeling* to the required style of writing.

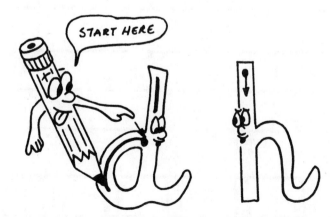

TRACING

Tracing is an important developmental stage toward helping the child produce his or her own letters. Tracing works on the principle of decreasing the visual stimulus of the letter trace from a solid line to the stage where only the starting and finishing points of the letter are given. The child has to trace along the line as accurately as possible. The letters should start off large in size with the lines to be traced thick; as the child shows efficiency at tracing, the letters can be reduced in size. (See the full-page sample.)

TRACING SAMPLE

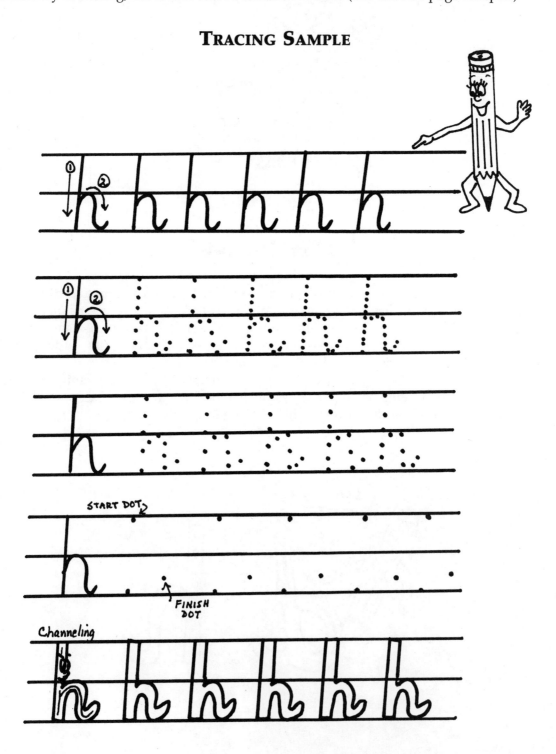

START DOT

FINISH DOT

Channeling

FADE-OUT

This technique is often used for dysgraphic children (children with severe handwriting difficulties). The principle of fading is based on progressively increasing the motor difficulty of the writing task while at the same time decreasing the visual stimuli that is presented to the child. An example of what the child must do is presented below. The fade-out alphabet can be found in Section 6.

FADE-OUT SAMPLE

Color these letters	*e*	*e*	*e*	*e*	*e*
Trace inside these letters	*e*	*e*	*e*	*e*	*e*
Trace along these letters	*e*	*e*	*e*	*e*	*e*
Trace along these letters	*e*	*e*	*e*	*e*	*e*
Trace along these letters					
Write your own letter					

Name _____

Complete Your Own Fade-Out:

Color these letters					
Trace inside these letters					
Trace along these letters					
Trace along these letters					
Trace along these letters					
Write your own letter					

TEACHING LETTER FORMATIONS

Here is an alternative method to use for teaching and practicing correct letter formation besides using colored lines or cartoon characters as described earlier in this section.

The teaching of letters should be made as simple as possible by grouping the letters in "families" based on their movement patterns as presented below.

1. The counterclockwise "c" family: **a, c, d, g, o, s, e**

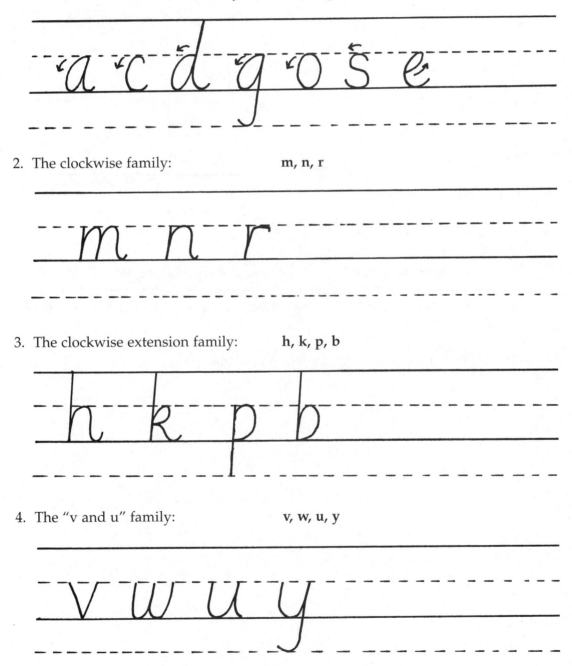

2. The clockwise family: **m, n, r**

3. The clockwise extension family: **h, k, p, b**

4. The "v and u" family: **v, w, u, y**

Note: Once the letters of a family have been learned, the children can then use them to make words; for example, dog.

5. The straight family: **i, j, l, t**

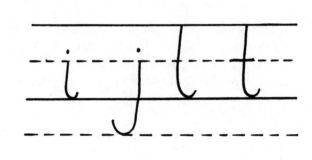

6. The "odd ones": **f, x**

These letter formations can be practiced using the pencil control activities of channeling and tracing as described earlier. Remember, an efficient grip needs to be established for the child to produce acceptable letter formations. Good teaching and patience are the key to success.

7. Use the reproducible on the next page on the next page to assess letter shapes.

Letter Shapes

Place a checkmark under each letter when the child can complete both the capital and lower case of the letter successfully.

Name	Aa	Bb	Cc	Dd	Ee	Ff	Gg	Hh	Ii	Jj	Kk	Ll	Mm	Nn	Oo	Pp	Qq	Rr	St	Tt	Uu	Vv	Ww	Xx	Yy	Zz

SPATIAL ASPECTS

1. To assist in the spatial elements of size and spacing, children should be familiar with the language of writing and the activities described in the section on language concepts, pages 154–161.

2. The use of sloping parallelograms can assist when dealing with individual letters.

3. Slope sheets can be placed under the paper to give the child a strong visual cue as to the required slope consistency.

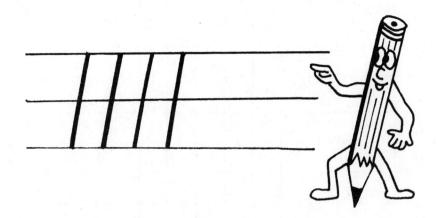

4. Pages that have dotted thirds are useful for children who are weak spatially. However, the children must be familiar with the lines; otherwise, many young children can actually become confused with all the lines because the page becomes too busy.

SPATIAL ASPECTS *(Continued)*

5. Children may overcome reversals by practicing these activities:

➤ Playing with the letters in an informal situation before formal writing begins.

➤ Visual discrimination activities.

➤ Spending more time on mirror-image letters.

➤ Reinforcing body image and spatial awareness activities, especially those exercises dealing with directionality.

➤ Kinesthetic exercises, such as sand tracing and raised letter tracing.

Lines are on the paper for a reason. You need to emphasize and reinforce that letters must touch the line. Children fail to touch lines because of lack of motor control; many fail to stay on lines because they rush their downstroke to the point where they cannot control it and either overshoot or do not reach the line. Tell children it is like going down a hill too fast on a bike or skateboard and having to turn a sharp corner. It's simply too hard!

LEGIBILITY

A number of factors determine whether or not writing appears legible. These include:

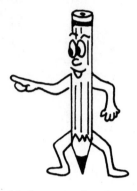

➤ Letter formation
➤ Slope of letters and their consistency
➤ Size consistency
➤ Spacing
➤ Individual style
➤ Positioning of letters with regard to lines

Perhaps one of the best ways to ensure that the child does not begin to write incorrect letter formations is to be aware of the common errors that young children make, which eventually lead to illegible writing. Correct the errors early so that they do not become exaggerated and habitual.

SUGGESTED GUIDELINES

1. Letters must be the correct height in relation to each other depending upon whether they are letters that have just a body, a head and a body, or a tail and a body.

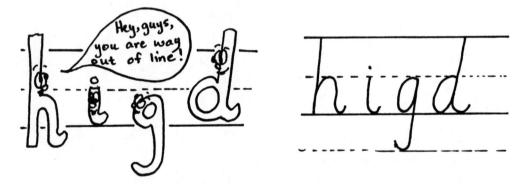

2. Closed letters such as "g" must be closed; otherwise, they look like another letter "y, a, u", etc.

SUGGESTED GUIDELINES *(Continued)*

3. Open letters must be open.

4. Straight strokes are straight: "i" can look like "c"; "v" like "u."

bin   bin

5. Curved strokes are curved; otherwise, the writing becomes very angular and difficult to read.

hm   him

6. Certain parts of letters to be joined *must* be joined; for example, "k."

back   back

SUGGESTED GUIDELINES *(Continued)*

7. All parts of letters should be seen: dots, crosses.

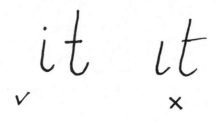

8. Spacing must be sufficient to recognize where one letter or word starts and another ends. Spacing is about the width of one letter.

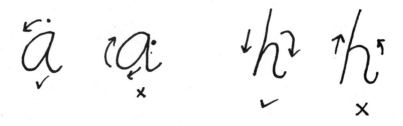

9. Letters have correct starting and finishing points. Most common errors are vertical strokes completed from the bottom upward, and counterclockwise movements completed in a clockwise direction.

10. Finish one letter before starting the next; otherwise, letters quickly lose their shape. For example, "a" becomes an "o."

11. Control the speed of writing so that the letters are correctly formed and the writing style is fluent and easily readable.

SUGGESTED GUIDELINES *(Continued)*

12. All downstrokes are parallel.

hill

13. All downstrokes are the same distance apart.

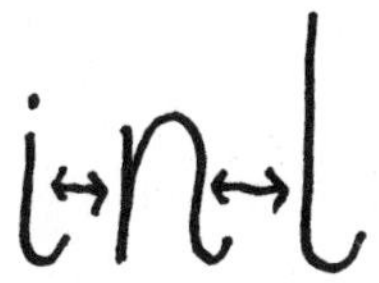

i↔n↔l

14. Letters that finish at the bottom of the marked line join with the next letter diagonally.

do   la

15. Letters that finish at the top of the marked line join with the next letter horizontally.

ora   bar

16. Use the reproducible on the following page to assess legibility.

LEGIBILITY

Place a C if correctly and consistently achieved.
Place an I if incorrectly and/or inconsistently achieved.

Name	Height	Letters closed	Letters open	Straight strokes	Curved strokes	Joins	Dots and crosses	Spacing	Down strokes parallel	Distance between downstrokes	Size of ascenders	Size of descenders

SPEED

Speed, or lack of it, can be due to a number of factors. However, before discussing these you need to be aware that children move with different levels of efficiency and there is a maximum speed at which they can write before control is sacrificed. What you must do with children is give them the necessary strategies to assist them in developing to their fullest potential.

STRATEGIES TO IMPROVE SPEED

1. *Fluency.* Young children tend to complete letters in segments, often stopping during the formation of a letter. The child who does this must be encouraged to write the letter in a single stroke. This can be achieved by having the children trace letters that have a distinct directional path, as illustrated below, so that the children can follow this path and complete the letter in the most efficient way. You can develop these yourself.

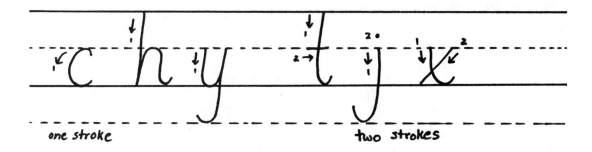

one stroke   two strokes

2. *Automation and Memory.* As memory and construction of letter formations develop and become automated, an increase in the speed of reproduction will follow. The simplest way to achieve this is through practice.

STRATEGIES TO IMPROVE SPEED *(Continued)*

3. *Tension.* Tension is one of the great destroyers of speed. The child needs to relax those body parts that are used in handwriting. Practicing scribbles will help the child relax the hand and write more fluently. Tension is also lessened when the adult is not placing too much pressure on the child.

4. *Incorrect Grip.* Incorrect grips, especially those that have more than just the index finger on top of the pencil, are notorious for slowing down writing.

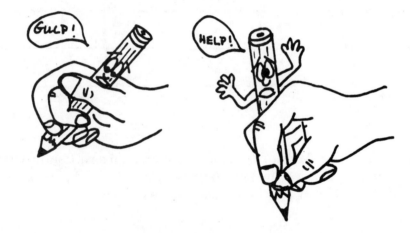

5. *Joins.* In the progressive development of the child's writing, although joins will assist in speeding up handwriting ability, they could result in the child going backward in terms of speed and legibility. Therefore, prepare the child for this and encourage him or her to continue with the change.

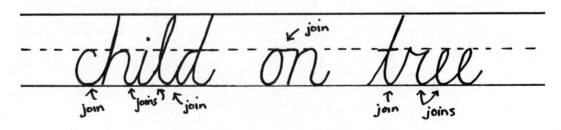

STRATEGIES TO IMPROVE SPEED *(Continued)*

6. *Speed Exercises.* Exercises can be used to promote speed and control. In the normal lesson, once a letter formation has been mastered, encourage the child to produce the letters faster. This can be achieved by having the first line of a page dedicated to the correct formation of a letter and the next line to producing the letter quickly while maintaining legibility.

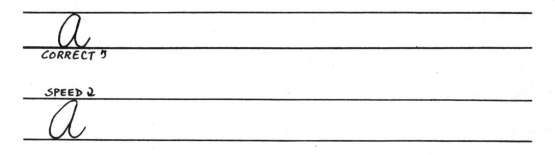

7. *Improve Arm Position.* If the writing arm is cramped into the side of the body, then fluency and speed are difficult.

8. *Allow Experimentation.* Children need to be allowed to experiment with different paper positions (within the correct framework) and writing implements to optimize their writing movements.

FINE-MOTOR/HANDWRITING ASSESSMENT

The following are examples of reports that have been completed on students with fine-motor and handwriting difficulties. Hopefully, these examples will provide some further insight as to some of the problems that children experience and will assist in student evaluations.

EXAMPLE 1

FINGER ISOLATION

Adam displayed a sound precision grip in all manipulative activities.

UNI-MANUAL COORDINATION (ONE-HANDED)

Adam performed this task well, scoring at the 80th percentile. He displayed good arm transport, and his grasp and release were efficient and accurate. Noticeable was the amount of head movement Adam displayed while performing this task. This did not affect his performance at this task, but excessive movements during some more precise tasks may affect his accuracy.

BI-MANUAL COORDINATION

Adam scored at the 90th percentile for this task, displaying accurate and efficient movements.

VISUAL-MOTOR INTEGRATION

Adam performed at an age-equivalent level for this task. This indicates that Adam has few difficulties in perceiving and integrating geometric shapes which then can often cause problems with handwriting skills.

Handwriting Skills

Many factors are integrated into handwriting skills. These include postural, motor, memory, visual, and attitudinal factors.

➤ *Body Posture*

Adam displays a very common problem when writing. Because he holds the pen too low, he tilts and lowers his head to the left to see what he is writing. This is not acceptable postural form because of the excessive strain to the eyes and poor positioning of the spine. This position will also likely have a negative impact on his writing. It was significant that Adam tilts his head more as his hand moves across the page.

➤ *Pencil Grip*

Although grips vary, there are certain characteristics that should be followed to ensure that Adam is best prepared for the demands that will be placed on his handwriting.

As stated earlier, the grip Adam uses is too low and too tight on the pencil. This will have the effect of slowing down his ability to write quickly. Adam also verbalized that his writing hand hurts while writing, especially if the period of time he has to write is of reasonable duration. To correct the position of his grip, place an elastic band on the pencil he uses at the desired distance from the tip. The actual grip construction is quite sound and should not be altered.

➤ *Support Hand*

Adam does not appear to consistently consider paper position or the position of his support hand. Both aspects are extremely important when handwriting as they affect body position, slope of letters, and stability of the paper while writing. Adam clenches his support hand into a fist and varies the position in which it is placed, often being positioned incorrectly. Adam also positions his paper too central to his body, whereby the paper is straight rather than angled with the top left-hand corner angled downward. Both factors may affect his formation and speed when writing.

➤ *Letter Construction*

Adam produced letter formations that were quite legible and the quality of his letters is good. Adam displays good wrist-and-finger action and his work has spatial consistency. For reasons due to paper positioning, his work does not have sufficient slope. The excessive pressure he places on the paper when writing may, in the long term, affect the quick and efficient joining of his letters. By using carbon paper under some of his written work and comparing it with what is expected, Adam will get instant visual feedback via the darkness of his carbon reproduction as to the amount of pressure he should be applying. If Adam is producing substandard work in class, it is most likely because he has to write too quickly than what he is at presently capable of, or he is not concentrating on the written task.

➤ *Speed*

Adam scored at the 20th percentile for speed. This is due primarily to his excessive grip and writing pressure as well as the positioning of his body.

COMMENTS

Adam displays difficulties in the execution of some locomotor tasks and needs to address some physical aspects of his handwriting. Adam displays difficulties remaining on task for any length of time and—as attention is the foundation of all learning—this is a problem that must be attended to immediately.

Time and patience are the key to improving Adam's coordination difficulties. Young children take much longer to master activities correctly than many think; therefore, the practicing of these activities must be consistent, encouraging, nonthreatening, and purposeful.

EXAMPLE 2

FINGER ISOLATION

Dane displayed some difficulties with finger isolation in both hands. The amount of concentration required to perform this simple task means that Dane is not giving attention to what should be a relatively automatic task. This means he cannot concentrate fully on other tasks that he may need to attend to.

PRECISION GRIP

Dane displayed some inconsistency in his precision grip, alternating between a four-finger grip, using the thumb and third finger only as well as the correct three-finger grip, although it is still quite acceptable for his age. Dane also displayed a slight amount of excessive tension in his finger movements which may affect accuracy in some tasks, especially writing. Teaching Dane to be aware of the tension when you observe it and then asking him to relax his fingers will be beneficial.

UNI-MANUAL COORDINATION (ONE-HANDED)

Dane performed this task very well, scoring at the 60th percentile. He displayed good arm transport, and Dane's grasp and release were efficient and accurate.

BI-MANUAL COORDINATION

Dane scored at the 60th percentile for this task. During the bead-stringing task, Dane continually changed hands to hold and thread, and this detracted from an even higher score. In these tasks there is increased importance on finger isolation and the added difficulty of requiring both sides of the body to work together.

VISUAL-MOTOR INTEGRATION

Dane scored at the 80th percentile with an age-equivalent score of 5 years 10 months. This indicates that Dane has no difficulties in perceiving and integrating geometric shapes, which can often cause problems with handwriting skills.

Handwriting Skills

Many factors are integrated into handwriting skills. These include postural, motor, memory, visual, and attitudinal factors. Although Dane will not commence formal writing until next year, some basic concepts of body position, grip, and basic arm movements are best established in pre-primary before bad habits become standard practice.

➤ *Body Posture*

Dane displays a very good posture. His back is straight and eyes are a good distance from the paper.

➤ *Pencil Grip*

Although grips vary, there are certain characteristics that should be followed to ensure that Dane is best prepared for the demands that will be placed on his handwriting. Dane has established a sound grip that will assist in his handwriting skills.

➤ *Support Hand*

Dane appears to consistently place his support hand in the proper position. Even at this stage when he is practicing writing, ensure that he tilts the paper at the correct angle.

➤ *Pencil Accuracy*

Dane displayed some difficulty with pencil-accuracy tasks. This is often a cause of handwriting difficulties in grade one children. I would suggest that tracing activities, dot-to-dot tasks, and maze activities are used with Dane to train this aspect of his pencil work. The cause of this inaccuracy is likely to be due to the tension that is evident in some of his manipulative work; Dane has yet to develop smooth arm movements from right to left as he writes, but this may develop with practice. At this stage Dane also produces his circles in the reverse direction; have him practice the correct direction (counterclockwise) as this is the direction that most of the letters follow.

➤ *Cutting Tasks*

When cutting, Dane has some difficulty in controlling the force of his cutting stroke. This is not uncommon at this age but practice at making small cuts and cuts of different sizes is a useful practice for the future. Dane also holds the paper he is cutting in an inconsistent manner—sometimes holding it vertically. Again, practice with Dane holding the paper correctly and moving the paper—*not* the scissors.

COMMENTS

Dane displays some difficulties in motor planning and in the execution of a number of physical tasks.

Some of his actions were impulsive. He did have problems attending to some of the motor tasks for any length of time. Time and patience are the key to improving Dane's coordination difficulties. Young children take much longer to master activities correctly than many think; therefore, the practicing of these activities must be consistent, encouraging, nonthreatening, and purposeful.

EXAMPLE 3

FINGER ISOLATION

Callan displayed little difficulty with finger isolation in both hands. Callan displayed some inconsistency in his precision grip, alternating between a four-finger grip, using the thumb and third finger only as well as the correct three-finger grip. This inconsistency was especially evident in the bi-manual (two-handed tasks) where he held the object too far back into the pads of his fingers instead of the fingertips, making manipulation more difficult.

UNI-MANUAL COORDINATION (ONE-HANDED)

Callan performed this task well, scoring at the 60th percentile. He displayed good arm transport, although his precision grip was inconsistent. Callan's grasp and release were efficient and accurate. It was interesting to note that Callan verbalized that he felt better using his left hand for this task and scored higher with this hand.

BI-MANUAL COORDINATION

Callan scored at the 80th percentile for this task, displaying accurate and efficient movements.

VISUAL-MOTOR INTEGRATION

Callan performed at an age-equivalent level for this task. This indicates that Callan has few difficulties in perceiving and integrating geometric shapes, which then can often cause problems with handwriting skills.

Handwriting Skills

Many factors are integrated into handwriting skills. These include postural, motor, memory, visual, and attitudinal factors.

➤ *Body Posture*

Callan displays a very common problem when writing. Because he holds the pen too low, he slightly tilts and lowers his head to the left to see what he is writing. This is not acceptable postural form because of the excessive strain to the eyes and poor positioning of the spine. This position will also likely have a negative impact on his writing. His writing arm is too far away from his body and quite poorly positioned. This will affect both speed and reproduction.

➤ *Pencil Grip*

Although grips vary, there are certain characteristics that should be followed to ensure that Callan is best prepared for the demands that will be placed on his handwriting.

As stated earlier, the grip Callan uses is too low on the pencil. To correct this, place an elastic band on the pencil he uses at the desired distance from the tip. The actual grip construction is quite sound and should not be altered.

➤ *Support Hand*

Callan does not appear to consistently consider paper position or the position of his support hand. Both aspects are extremely important when handwriting as they affect body position, slope of letters, and stability of the paper while writing. Callan positions his support hand at the bottom left-hand corner of the page and, as a consequence, the paper tends to move at times while he is writing.

Callan also positions his paper too far to the left of his body; the paper is straight rather than angled with the top left-hand corner angled downward. Both factors may affect his formation and speed when writing.

➤ *Letter Construction*

Callan produces letter formations that are quite legible although the quality of his letters are not smooth. Callan displays good wrist-and-finger action. His work has spatial consistency. For reasons due to paper positioning, his work does not have sufficient slope. He does appear to have some difficulty in producing consistent curved shapes, possibly a consequence of his positioning.

➤ *Speed*

Callan scored at the 45th percentile for speed. Were it not for an obvious copying problem, he would have scored higher.

COMMENTS

Callan was attentive and performed the tasks required of him enthusiastically. His manipulative skills are well developed, but his handwriting is adversely affected due to poor habits. It is important that these are quickly corrected so as not to become engrained. I feel with these adjustments, Callan will have little difficulty in coping with handwriting in the future.

WRITING STRATEGIES FOR LEFT-HANDERS

Many children experiencing writing difficulties are left-handed. This is to be expected because the directional and structural components of handwriting have been developed to accommodate right-handers. Left-handers have to write against the natural flow of their hand, so we need to give them strategies that will assist in acquiring proficient techniques.

Tip: Don't sit a left-handed child next to a right-handed child!

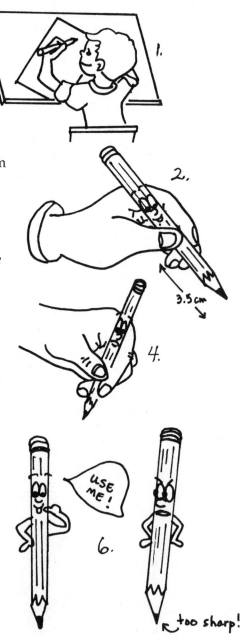

1. The left-hander should sit higher on the chair than a right-hander. This will help the child see what he or she is writing.

2. The grip for the left-hander should be higher up the pencil than the right-hander (approximately 3.5 cms or 1-1/2 inches from the tip).

3. The common hooked wrist should be strongly discouraged. The left-hander should be encouraged to write from the *side* of the line, not from the top or from underneath the line.

4. The grip pressure of a left-hander should be equal among the thumb, middle, and index finger to keep the pen low in the hand.

5. Paper position is important. The page should be left of center with the top right-hand corner of the page sloping downward.

6. Left-handers beginning to write should use soft leads that are not too sharp. This will allow the pencil to glide over the page easily.

STRATEGIES FOR WORKING WITH PARENTS OF CHILDREN WITH COORDINATION DIFFICULTIES

MAKING CONTACT WITH PARENTS

It is inevitable that some children will experience significant difficulties in the area of movement. Contacting the parents of these children is perhaps the most involved form of contact that is required of the teacher. Here are some guidelines to follow.

➤ Do not wait to contact parents about a problem until it is too late. Parents have the right to become annoyed if they are contacted late in the year about a problem that should have been picked up earlier.

➤ Make initial contact by telephone.

➤ Do not talk about *problems;* it is better to refer to them as *difficulties.*

➤ Ask the parents if they notice anything about their child's coordination, rather than expand on all their child's problems. Some parents are "ego bound" in their children and see their child's failures as a reflection of themselves. Therefore, they have difficulties coping with a barrage of negative information.

➤ Suggest that parent(s) come into the class as a helper and observe their child in comparison with other children. Then ask again what differences they notice.

➤ Give parents the opportunity to discuss and think about the information provided in this initial contact, and suggest that another telephone call or meeting be held in the near future. Ongoing contact between both parties then becomes essential to coordinate efforts to assist the child.

➤ Ensure that you have all the available information on the child's physical development at the time of initial contact. Observational assessment is useful, but it may also be helpful to have some concrete information in the form of standardized test results. A simple-to-administer test, such as the "Stay in Step" (see Resources Index for details) combined with observational material, provides you with enough information to give the parents an insight into the problems their child faces.

➤ After the initial contact, send parents written information, reinforcing what was discussed on the phone.

➤ Once you see that the parents are aware of a difficulty, you should be positive, highlighting the attributes at which the child has had success. Then discuss the difficulties that the child is experiencing.

Note: You should not feel guilty about a child's problems. Coordination difficulties have been developing from a young age. In contacting the parents early, you are following the best procedure, both ethically and professionally. Some parents may understandably become upset, so this is where the skills of active listening are very useful. If parents become aggressive, bring the discussion down to a factual level, and emphasize what **we can do** to help the child. Finally, if more than one teacher is involved in the contact, ensure that collaboration and a strategic plan between the teachers has been established before contact.

SECTION 6

HANDWRITING ACTIVITIES

This section provides you with two styles of alphabet handwriting:

➤ *Manuscript* and *Cursive* for Northern Hemisphere **(NH)** countries like the United States, and Canada.

➤ *Modern Cursive* for Southern Hemisphere **(SH)** countries like Australia. For your reference, the alphabet charts are provided at the end of Section 6 along with blank practice pages. (See pages 290-295.) **NH** and **SH** on the writing activities distinguish the alphabets for you.

The first two pages of the section demonstrate correct and incorrect pencil grips for right- and left-handed people. Once students have mastered pencil grips, you can then move to the Channeling and Fade-Out Alphabet activities that provide numerous opportunities to practice tracing and writing the alphabet.

Each alphabet style follows the same predictable format:

➤ Channeling Activity for the lower case letters

➤ Fade-Out Activities for lower case letters

➤ Fade-Out Activities for upper case letters

An entire page is devoted to practicing most of the lower case alphabets since much of our writing consists of these letters. The upper case letters are grouped together on several pages.

The Channeling Activity provides easy practice in following the letter flow of the lower case alphabet. Amusing faces on the letters keep beginners interested and motivated to write. The Fade-Out Activities ask students to color letters, to trace inside them, and then to trace along them by following whole and broken lines. The last part asks students to write the letter on their own using a start point. The color-trace-write progression gives students practice as well as confidence with their writing skills.

You can present the practice pages to students in any order you wish and as many times as you think necessary. Each page can be easily reproduced on a copier for individual, small group, or whole class use. NOTE: If a student experiences frustration with a letter after several practices, you may need to move on to the next letter activity and then revisit this one at an opportune time.

If, for some reason, you are unable to use these letters, the reproducible activities in this section should provide a valuable example of how to produce your own worksheets.

RIGHT-HAND PENCIL GRIPS

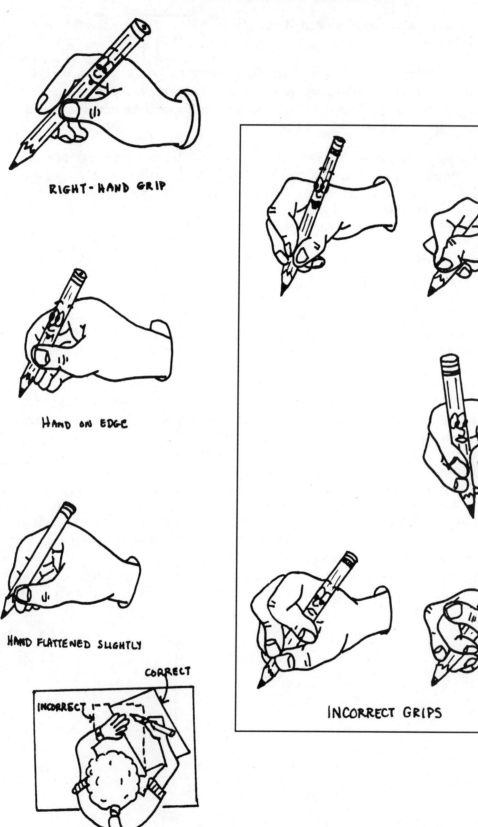

RIGHT-HAND GRIP

HAND ON EDGE

HAND FLATTENED SLIGHTLY

CORRECT

INCORRECT

INCORRECT GRIPS

LEFT-HAND PENCIL GRIPS

CORRECT LEFT-HAND
GRIP

CORRECT

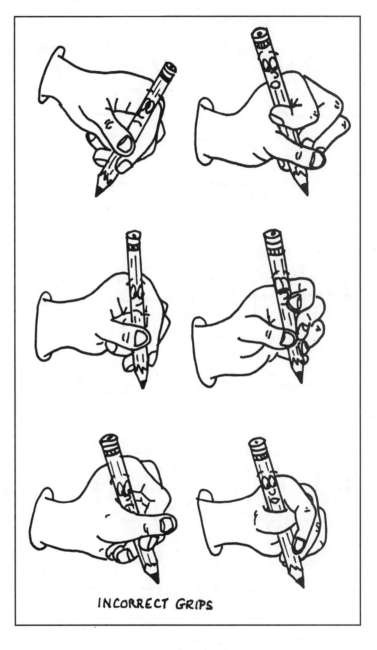

INCORRECT GRIPS

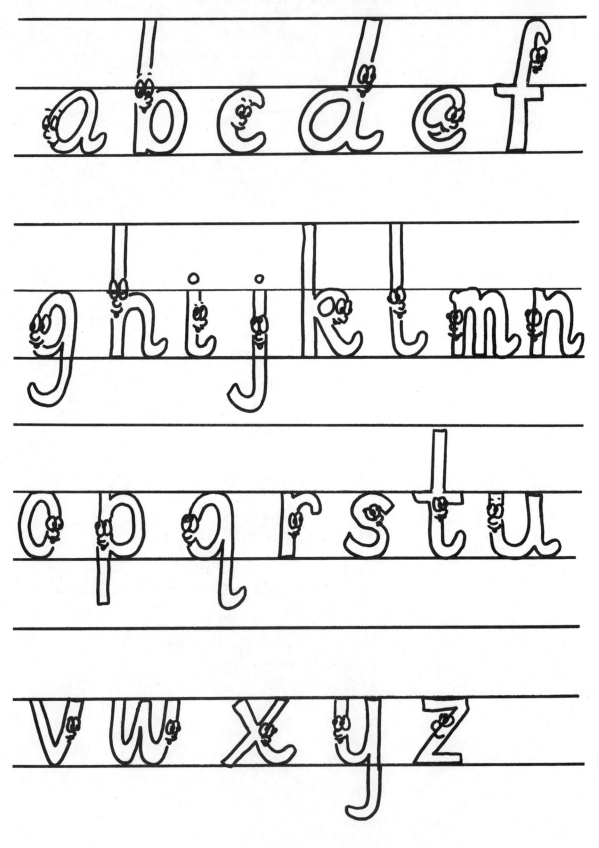

Complete your own Fade-Out page.

Lower Case Manuscript (NH)

Color these letters	a	a	a	a	a
Trace inside these letters	a	a	a	a	a
Trace along these letters	a	a	a	a	a
Trace along these letters	a	a	a	a	a
Trace along these letters					
Write your own letter					

Name _____   Date _____

Complete your own Fade-Out page.

Color these letters	b	b	b	b	b
Trace inside these letters	b	b	b	b	b
Trace along these letters	b	b	b	b	b
Trace along these letters	b	b	b	b	b
Trace along these letters	b	b	b	b	b
Write your own letter					

Name _____ Date _____

Complete your own Fade-Out page.

Lower Case Manuscript (NH)

Color these letters	c	c	c	c	c
Trace inside these letters	c	c	c	c	c
Trace along these letters	c	c	c	c	c
Trace along these letters	c	c	c	c	c
Trace along these letters					
Write your own letter					

Name _____ **Date** _____

Complete your own Fade-Out page.

Color these letters	d	d	d	d	d
Trace inside these letters	d	d	d	d	d
Trace along these letters	d	d	d	d	d
Trace along these letters					
Trace along these letters					
Write your own letter					

Name _____   Date _____

Complete your own Fade-Out page.

Color these letters	e	e	e	e	e
Trace inside these letters	e	e	e	e	e
Trace along these letters	e	e	e	e	e
Trace along these letters					
Trace along these letters					
Write your own letter					

Name _____   Date _____

Complete your own Fade-Out page.

Color these letters	f	f	f	f	f
Trace inside these letters	f	f	f	f	f
Trace along these letters	f	f	f	f	f
Trace along these letters	f	f	f	f	f
Trace along these letters	f	f	f	f	f
Write your own letter					

Name _____ Date _____

Complete your own Fade-Out page.

Color these letters	*g*	*g*	*g*	*g*	*g*
Trace inside these letters	*g*	*g*	*g*	*g*	*g*
Trace along these letters	*g*	*g*	*g*	*g*	*g*
Trace along these letters	*g*	*g*	*g*	*g*	*g*
Trace along these letters					
Write your own letter					

Name _____   Date _____

Complete your own Fade-Out page.

Color these letters	h	h	h	h	h
Trace inside these letters	h	h	h	h	h
Trace along these letters	h	h	h	h	h
Trace along these letters					
Trace along these letters					
Write your own letter					

Name _____ Date _____

Complete your own Fade-Out page.

Lower Case Manuscript (NH)

Color these letters	i	i	i	i	i
Trace inside these letters	i	i	i	i	i
Trace along these letters	i	i	i	i	i
Trace along these letters	i	i	i	i	i
Trace along these letters	i	i	i	i	i
Write your own letter					

Name _____   Date _____

Complete your own Fade-Out page.

Color these letters					
Trace inside these letters					
Trace along these letters					
Trace along these letters					
Trace along these letters					
Write your own letter					

Name _____ Date _____

Complete your own Fade-Out page.

Lower Case Manuscript (NH)

Color these letters	k	k	k	k	k
Trace inside these letters	k	k	k	k	k
Trace along these letters	k	k	k	k	k
Trace along these letters	k	k	k	k	k
Trace along these letters					
Write your own letter					

Name _____   Date _____

Complete your own Fade-Out page.

Lower Case Manuscript (NH)

Color these letters					
Trace inside these letters					
Trace along these letters					
Trace along these letters					
Trace along these letters					
Write your own letter					

© 1999 by Joanne M. Landy & Keith R. Burridge

Name _____ Date _____

Complete your own Fade-Out page.

Lower Case Manuscript (NH)

Color these letters	m	m	m	m	m
Trace inside these letters	m	m	m	m	m
Trace along these letters	m	m	m	m	m
Trace along these letters	m	m	m	m	m
Trace along these letters					
Write your own letter					

Name _____ **Date** _____

Complete your own Fade-Out page.

Color these letters	n	n	n	n	n
Trace inside these letters	n	n	n	n	n
Trace along these letters	n	n	n	n	n
Trace along these letters	n	n	n	n	n
Trace along these letters					
Write your own letter					

Name _____ Date _____

Complete your own Fade-Out page.

Lower Case Manuscript (NH)

Color these letters	O	O	O	O	O
Trace inside these letters	O	O	O	O	O
Trace along these letters	O	O	O	O	O
Trace along these letters	○	○	○	○	○
Trace along these letters					
Write your own letter					

Name _____   Date _____

Complete your own Fade-Out page.

Color these letters	P	P	P	P	P
Trace inside these letters	P	P	P	P	P
Trace along these letters	P	P	P	P	P
Trace along these letters	P	P	P	P	P
Trace along these letters					
Write your own letter					

Name _____ Date _____

Complete your own Fade-Out page.

Color these letters	q	q	q	q	q
Trace inside these letters	q	q	q	q	q
Trace along these letters	q	q	q	q	q
Trace along these letters	q	q	q	q	q
Trace along these letters					
Write your own letter					

Name _____   Date _____

Complete your own Fade-Out page.

Color these letters	r	r	r	r	r
Trace inside these letters	r	r	r	r	r
Trace along these letters	r	r	r	r	r
Trace along these letters	r	r	r	r	r
Trace along these letters	r	r	r	r	r
Write your own letter					

Name _____ Date _____

Complete your own Fade-Out page.

Lower Case Manuscript (NH)

Color these letters	S	S	S	S	S
Trace inside these letters	S	S	S	S	S
Trace along these letters	S	S	S	S	S
Trace along these letters	s	s	s	s	s
Trace along these letters					
Write your own letter					

Name _____   Date _____

Complete your own Fade-Out page.

Color these letters	t	t	t	t	t
Trace inside these letters	t	t	t	t	t
Trace along these letters	t	t	t	t	t
Trace along these letters	t	t	t	t	t
Trace along these letters	t	t	t	t	t
Write your own letter					

Name _____   **Date** _____

Complete your own Fade-Out page.

Color these letters	u	u	u	u	u
Trace inside these letters	u	u	u	u	u
Trace along these letters	u	u	u	u	u
Trace along these letters	u	u	u	u	u
Trace along these letters					
Write your own letter					

Name _____   Date _____

Complete your own Fade-Out page.

Color these letters	V	V	V	V	V
Trace inside these letters	V	V	V	V	V
Trace along these letters	V	V	V	V	V
Trace along these letters	v	v	v	v	v
Trace along these letters	v	v	v	v	v
Write your own letter	v	v	v	v	v

Name  **Date** _____

Complete your own Fade-Out page.

Lower Case Manuscript (NH)

Color these letters	⣌	⣌	⣌	⣌	⣌
Trace inside these letters	⣌	⣌	⣌	⣌	⣌
Trace along these letters	w	w	w	w	w
Trace along these letters	⣌	⣌	⣌	⣌	⣌
Trace along these letters	⣌	⣌	⣌	⣌	⣌
Write your own letter					

Name _____   Date _____

Complete your own Fade-Out page.

Color these letters	X	X	X	X	X
Trace inside these letters	X	X	X	X	X
Trace along these letters	X	X	X	X	X
Trace along these letters	X	X	X	X	X
Trace along these letters					
Write your own letter					

Name _____ Date _____

Complete your own Fade-Out page.

Lower Case Manuscript (NH)

Color these letters	y	y	y	y	y
Trace inside these letters	y	y	y	y	y
Trace along these letters	y	y	y	y	y
Trace along these letters	y	y	y	y	y
Trace along these letters	y	y	y	y	y
Write your own letter					

Name _____   Date _____

Complete your own Fade-Out page.

Color these letters	Z	Z	Z	Z	Z
Trace inside these letters	Z	Z	Z	Z	Z
Trace along these letters	Z	Z	Z	Z	Z
Trace along these letters	z	z	z	z	z
Trace along these letters					
Write your own letter					

Name _____   Date _____

Complete your own Fade-Out page.

Color these letters	A	B	C	D	E
Trace inside these letters	A	B	C	D	E
Trace along these letters	A	B	C	D	E
Trace along these letters	A	B	C	D	E
Trace along these letters					
Write your own letter					

Name _____ Date _____

Complete your own Fade-Out page.

Color these letters	F	G	H	I	J
Trace inside these letters	F	G	H	I	J
Trace along these letters	F	G	H	I	J
Trace along these letters					
Trace along these letters					
Write your own letter					

Name _____ **Date** _____

Complete your own Fade-Out page.

Color these letters	K	L	M	N	O
Trace inside these letters	K	L	M	N	O
Trace along these letters	K	L	M	N	O
Trace along these letters	K	L	M	N	O
Trace along these letters	K	L	M	N	O
Write your own letter					

Name _____   Date _____

Complete your own Fade-Out page.

Color these letters	P	Q	R	S	T
Trace inside these letters	P	Q	R	S	T
Trace along these letters	P	Q	R	S	T
Trace along these letters	P	Q	R	S	T
Trace along these letters					
Write your own letter					

Name _____   Date _____

Complete your own Fade-Out page.

Upper Case Manuscript (NH)

Color these letters	U	V	W	X	Y
Trace inside these letters	U	V	W	X	Y
Trace along these letters	U	V	W	X	Y
Trace along these letters					
Trace along these letters					
Write your own letter					

Name _____   **Date** _____

Complete your own Fade-Out page.

Color these letters	Z				
Trace inside these letters	Z				
Trace along these letters	Z				
Trace along these letters	Z				
Trace along these letters	Z				
Write your own letter					

© 1999 by Joanne M. Landy & Keith R. Burridge

Name _____ **Date** _____

Complete your own Fade-Out page.

Color these letters	*a*	*b*	*c*	*d*	*e*
Trace inside these letters	*a*	*b*	*c*	*d*	*e*
Trace along these letters	*a*	*b*	*c*	*d*	*e*
Trace along these letters	*a*	*b*	*c*	*d*	*e*
Trace along these letters					
Write your own letter					

Name _____   Date _____

Complete your own Fade-Out page.

Color these letters	*f*	*g*	*h*	*i*	*j*
Trace inside these letters	*f*	*g*	*h*	*i*	*j*
Trace along these letters	*f*	*g*	*h*	*i*	*j*
Trace along these letters	*f*	*g*	*h*	*i*	*j*
Trace along these letters					
Write your own letter					

Name _____   **Date** _____

Complete your own Fade-Out page.

Color these letters	*k*	*l*	*m*	*n*	*o*
Trace inside these letters	*k*	*l*	*m*	*n*	*o*
Trace along these letters	*k*	*l*	*m*	*n*	*o*
Trace along these letters	*k*	*l*	*m*	*n*	*o*
Trace along these letters					
Write your own letter					

Name _____   Date _____

Complete your own Fade-Out page.

Color these letters	*p*	*q*	*r*	*s*	*t*
Trace inside these letters	*p*	*q*	*r*	*s*	*t*
Trace along these letters	*p*	*q*	*r*	*s*	*t*
Trace along these letters	*p*	*q*	*r*	*s*	*t*
Trace along these letters					
Write your own letter					

Name _____   Date _____

Complete your own Fade-Out page.

Color these letters	u	v	w	x	y
Trace inside these letters	u	v	w	x	y
Trace along these letters	u	v	w	x	y
Trace along these letters	u	v	w	x	y
Trace along these letters					
Write your own letter					

Name _____ Date _____

Complete your own Fade-Out page.

Color these letters					
Trace inside these letters					
Trace along these letters					
Trace along these letters					
Trace along these letters					
Write your own letter					

Name _____   Date _____

Complete your own Fade-Out page.

Color these letters	*A*	*B*	*C*	*D*	*E*
Trace inside these letters	*A*	*B*	*C*	*D*	*E*
Trace along these letters	*A*	*B*	*C*	*D*	*E*
Trace along these letters	*A*	*B*	*C*	*D*	*E*
Trace along these letters					
Write your own letter					

Name _____   Date _____

Complete your own Fade-Out page.

Color these letters	*F*	*G*	*H*	*I*	*J*
Trace inside these letters	*F*	*G*	*H*	*I*	*J*
Trace along these letters	*F*	*G*	*H*	*I*	*J*
Trace along these letters					
Trace along these letters					
Write your own letter					

Name _____ Date _____

Complete your own Fade-Out page.

Color these letters	K	L	m	n	O
Trace inside these letters	K	L	m	n	O
Trace along these letters	K	L	m	n	O
Trace along these letters	K	L	m	n	O
Trace along these letters					
Write your own letter					

Name _____   Date _____

Complete your own Fade-Out page.

Color these letters	P	2	R	S	T
Trace inside these letters	P	2	R	S	T
Trace along these letters	P	2	R	S	T
Trace along these letters	P	2	R	S	T
Trace along these letters					
Write your own letter					

Name _____   Date _____

Complete your own Fade-Out page.

Color these letters	U	V	W	X	Y
Trace inside these letters	U	V	W	X	Y
Trace along these letters	U	V	W	X	Y
Trace along these letters	U	V	W	X	Y
Trace along these letters	U	V	W	X	Y
Write your own letter					

Name _____   Date _____

Complete your own Fade-Out page.

Color these letters					
Trace inside these letters					
Trace along these letters					
Trace along these letters					
Trace along these letters					
Write your own letter					

Name _____   Date _____

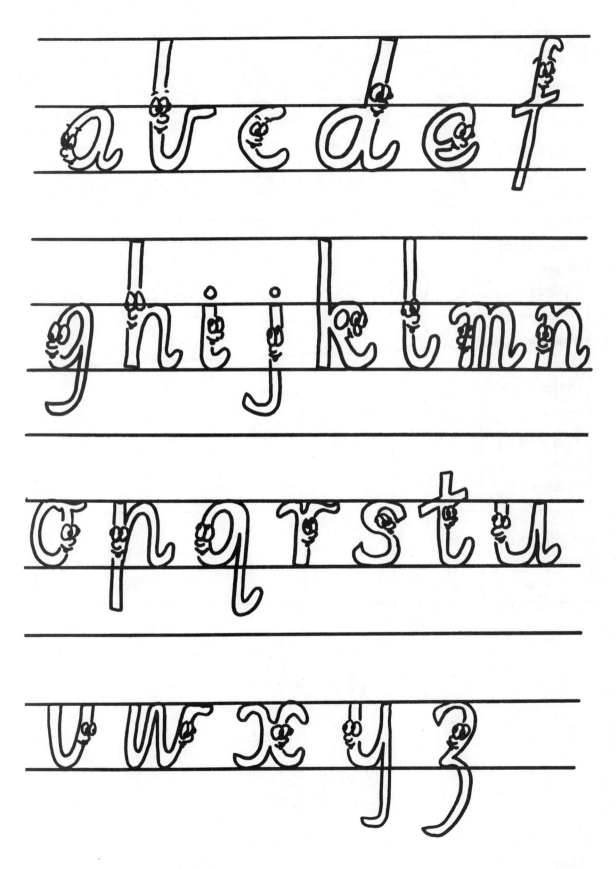

Complete your own Fade-Out page.

Lower Case Modern Cursive (SH)

Color these letters	𝑎	𝑎	𝑎	𝑎	𝑎
Trace inside these Letters	𝑎	𝑎	𝑎	𝑎	𝑎
Trace along these Letters	ä	ä	ä	ä	ä
Trace along these Letters					
Trace along these Letters					
Write your own letter					

Name _____   Date _____

Complete your own Fade-Out page.

Lower Case Modern Cursive (SH)

Color these letters					
Trace inside these letters					
Trace along these letters					
Trace along these letters					
Trace along these letters					
Write your own letter					

Name _____ **Date** _____

Complete your own Fade-Out page.

Color these letters	C	C	C	C	C
Trace inside these letters	C	C	C	C	C
Trace along these letters	C	C	C	C	C
Trace along these letters					
Trace along these letters					
Write your own letter					

Name _____ Date _____

Complete your own Fade-Out page.

Lower Case Modern Cursive (SH)

Color these letters	d	d	d	d	d
Trace inside these letters	d	d	d	d	d
Trace along these letters	d	d	d	d	d
Trace along these letters	d	d	d	d	d
Trace along these letters					
Write your own letter					

Name _____ Date _____

Complete your own Fade-Out page.

Color these letters	*e*	*e*	*e*	*e*	*e*
Trace inside these letters	*e*	*e*	*e*	*e*	*e*
Trace along these letters	*e*	*e*	*e*	*e*	*e*
Trace along these letters	*e*	*e*	*e*	*e*	*e*
Trace along these letters	*e*	*e*	*e*	*e*	*e*
Write your own letter	.	.	.	.	.

Name _____   Date _____

Complete your own Fade-Out page.

Lower Case Modern Cursive (SH)

Color these letters	*f*	*f*	*f*	*f*	*f*
Trace inside these letters	*f*	*f*	*f*	*f*	*f*
Trace along these letters	*f*	*f*	*f*	*f*	*f*
Trace along these letters					
Trace along these letters					
Write your own letter					

Name _____   Date _____

Complete your own Fade-Out page.

Lower Case Modern Cursive (SH)

Color these letters	9	9	9	9	9
Trace inside these letters	9	9	9	9	9
Trace along these letters	9	9	9	9	9
Trace along these letters	9	9	9	9	9
Trace along these letters					
Write your own letter					

Name _____ **Date** _____

Complete your own Fade-Out page.

Lower Case Modern Cursive (SH)

Color these letters	h	h	h	h	h
Trace inside these letters	h	h	h	h	h
Trace along these letters	h	h	h	h	h
Trace along these letters	h	h	h	h	h
Trace along these letters	h	h	h	h	h
Write your own letter					

Name _____   **Date** _____

Complete your own Fade-Out page.

Lower Case Modern Cursive (SH)

Color these letters	i	i	i	i	i
Trace inside these letters	i	i	i	i	i
Trace along these letters	i	i	i	i	i
Trace along these letters	i	i	i	i	i
Trace along these letters	i	i	i	i	i
Write your own letter	↓•	↓•	↓•	↓•	↓•

Name _____   Date _____

Complete your own Fade-Out page.

Lower Case Modern Cursive (SH)

Color these letters	j	j	j	j	j
Trace inside these letters	↓j	↓j	↓j	↓j	↓j
Trace along these letters	↓j	↓j	↓j	↓j	↓j
Trace along these letters	↓j	↓j	↓j	↓j	↓j
Trace along these letters	↓j	↓j	↓j	↓j	↓j
Write your own letter	↓•	↓•	↓•	↓•	↓•

Name _____   Date _____

Complete your own Fade-Out page.

Color these letters	k	k	k	k	k
Trace inside these letters	k	k	k	k	k
Trace along these letters	k	k	k	k	k
Trace along these letters	k	k	k	k	k
Trace along these letters					
Write your own letter					

Name _____   Date _____

Complete your own Fade-Out page.

Lower Case Modern Cursive (SH)

Color these letters					
Trace inside these letters					
Trace along these letters					
Trace along these letters					
Trace along these letters					
Write your own letter					

© 1999 by Joanne M. Landy & Keith R. Burridge

Name _____   Date _____

Complete your own Fade-Out page.

Lower Case Modern Cursive (SH)

Color these letters	m	m	m	m	m
Trace inside these letters	m	m	m	m	m
Trace along these letters	m	m	m	m	m
Trace along these letters	m	m	m	m	m
Trace along these letters	m	m	m	m	m
Write your own letter					

Name _____ **Date** _____

Complete your own Fade-Out page.

Lower Case Modern Cursive (SH)

Color these letters	n	n	n	n	n
Trace inside these letters	n	n	n	n	n
Trace along these letters	n	n	n	n	n
Trace along these letters	n	n	n	n	n
Trace along these letters					
Write your own letter					

Name _____ Date _____

Complete your own Fade-Out page.

Lower Case Modern Cursive (SH)

Color these letters					
Trace inside these Letters					
Trace along these Letters					
Trace along these Letters					
Trace along these Letters					
Write your own letter					

© 1999 by Joanne M. Landy & Keith R. Burridge

Name _____ **Date** _____

Complete your own Fade-Out page.

Color these letters	h	h	h	h	h
Trace inside these letters	↓ h	↓ h	↓ h	↓ h	↓ h
Trace along these letters	↓ ∩	↓ ∩	↓ ∩	↓ ∩	↓ ∩
Trace along these letters	↓	↓	↓	↓	↓
Trace along these letters	↓	↓	↓	↓	↓
Write your own letter	↓	↓	↓	↓	↓

Name _____   Date _____

Complete your own Fade-Out page.

Lower Case Modern Cursive (SH)

Color these letters	q	q	q	q	q
Trace inside these letters	q	q	q	q	q
Trace along these letters	q	q	q	q	q
Trace along these letters	q	q	q	q	q
Trace along these letters					
Write your own letter					

Name _____   **Date** _____

Complete your own Fade-Out page. Lower Case Modern Cursive (SH)

Color these letters					
Color these letters					
Trace inside these letters					
Trace along these letters					
Trace along these letters					
Trace along these letters					
Write your own letter					

Name _____ **Date** _____

Complete your own Fade-Out page.

Lower Case Modern Cursive (SH)

Color these letters	S	S	S	S	S
Trace inside these letters	S	S	S	S	S
Trace along these letters	S	S	S	S	S
Trace along these letters	S	S	S	S	S
Trace along these letters					
Write your own letter					

Name _____   Date _____

Complete your own Fade-Out page.

Lower Case Modern Cursive (SH)

Color these letters	t	t	t	t	t
Trace inside these letters	t	t	t	t	t
Trace along these letters	t	t	t	t	t
Trace along these letters					
Trace along these letters					
Write your own letter					

Name _____   Date _____

Complete your own Fade-Out page.

Color these letters	u	u	u	u	u
Trace inside these letters	u	u	u	u	u
Trace along these letters	u	u	u	u	u
Trace along these letters	u	u	u	u	u
Trace along these letters					
Write your own letter					

Name _____   Date _____

Complete your own Fade-Out page.

Lower Case Modern Cursive (SH)

Color these letters	U	U	U	U	U
Trace inside these letters	U	U	U	U	U
Trace along these letters	U	U	U	U	U
Trace along these letters	U	U	U	U	U
Trace along these letters					
Write your own letter					

Name _____ Date _____

Complete your own Fade-Out page.

Color these letters	w	w	w	w	w
Trace inside these letters	w	w	w	w	w
Trace along these letters	w	w	w	w	w
Trace along these letters	w	w	w	w	w
Trace along these letters					
Write your own letter					

Name _____   **Date** _____

Complete your own Fade-Out page.

Lower Case Modern Cursive (SH)

Color these letters					
Trace inside these letters					
Trace along these letters					
Trace along these letters					
Trace along these letters					
Write your own letter					

Name _____ **Date** _____

Complete your own Fade-Out page.

Lower Case Modern Cursive (SH)

Color these letters	y	y	y	y	y
Trace inside these letters	↓ y	↓ y	↓ y	↓ y	↓ y
Trace along these letters	↓ y	↓ y	↓ y	↓ y	↓ y
Trace along these letters	↓	↓	↓	↓	↓
Trace along these letters	↓	↓	↓	↓	↓
Write your own letter	↓	↓	↓	↓	↓

Name _____   Date _____

Complete your own Fade-Out page.   Lower Case Modern Cursive (SH)

Color these letters	3	3	3	3	3
Trace inside these letters	3	3	3	3	3
Trace along these letters	3	3	3	3	3
Trace along these letters	3	3	3	3	3
Trace along these letters					
Write your own letter					

Name _____   Date _____

Complete your own Fade-Out page.

Color these letters	A	B	C	D	E
Trace inside these letters	A	B	C	D	E
Trace along these letters	A	B	C	D	E
Trace along these letters	A	B	C	D	E
Trace along these letters	A	B	C	D	E
Write your own letter					

Name _____   Date _____

Complete your own Fade-Out page.   Upper Case Modern Cursive (SH)

Color these letters	F	G	H	I	J
Trace inside these letters	F	G	H	I	J
Trace along these letters	F	G	H	I	J
Trace along these letters	F	G	H	I	J
Trace along these letters					
Write your own letter					

Name _____   **Date** _____

Complete your own Fade-Out page.

Upper Case Modern Cursive (SH)

Color these letters	K	L	M	N	O
Trace inside these letters	K	L	M	N	O
Trace along these letters	K	L	M	N	O
Trace along these letters	K	L	M	N	O
Trace along these letters					
Write your own letter					

Name _____   Date _____

Complete your own Fade-Out page.

Upper Case Modern Cursive (SH)

Color these letters	P	Q	R	S	T
Trace inside these letters	P	Q	R	S	T
Trace along these letters	P	Q	R	S	T
Trace along these letters	P	Q	R	S	T
Trace along these letters	P	Q	R	S	T
Write your own letter					

Name _____ **Date** _____

Complete your own Fade-Out page.

Upper Case Modern Cursive (SH)

Color these letters	U	V	W	X	Y
Trace inside these letters	U	V	W	X	Y
Trace along these letters	U	V	W	X	Y
Trace along these letters	U	V	W	X	Y
Trace along these letters					
Write your own letter					

Name _____ Date _____

Complete your own Fade-Out page.

Upper Case Modern Cursive (SH)

Color these letters	Z				
Trace inside these letters	Z				
Trace along these letters	Z				
Trace along these letters	Z				
Trace along these letters	Z				
Write your own letter					

Name _____ Date _____

Lower and Upper Case Manuscript Chart (NH)

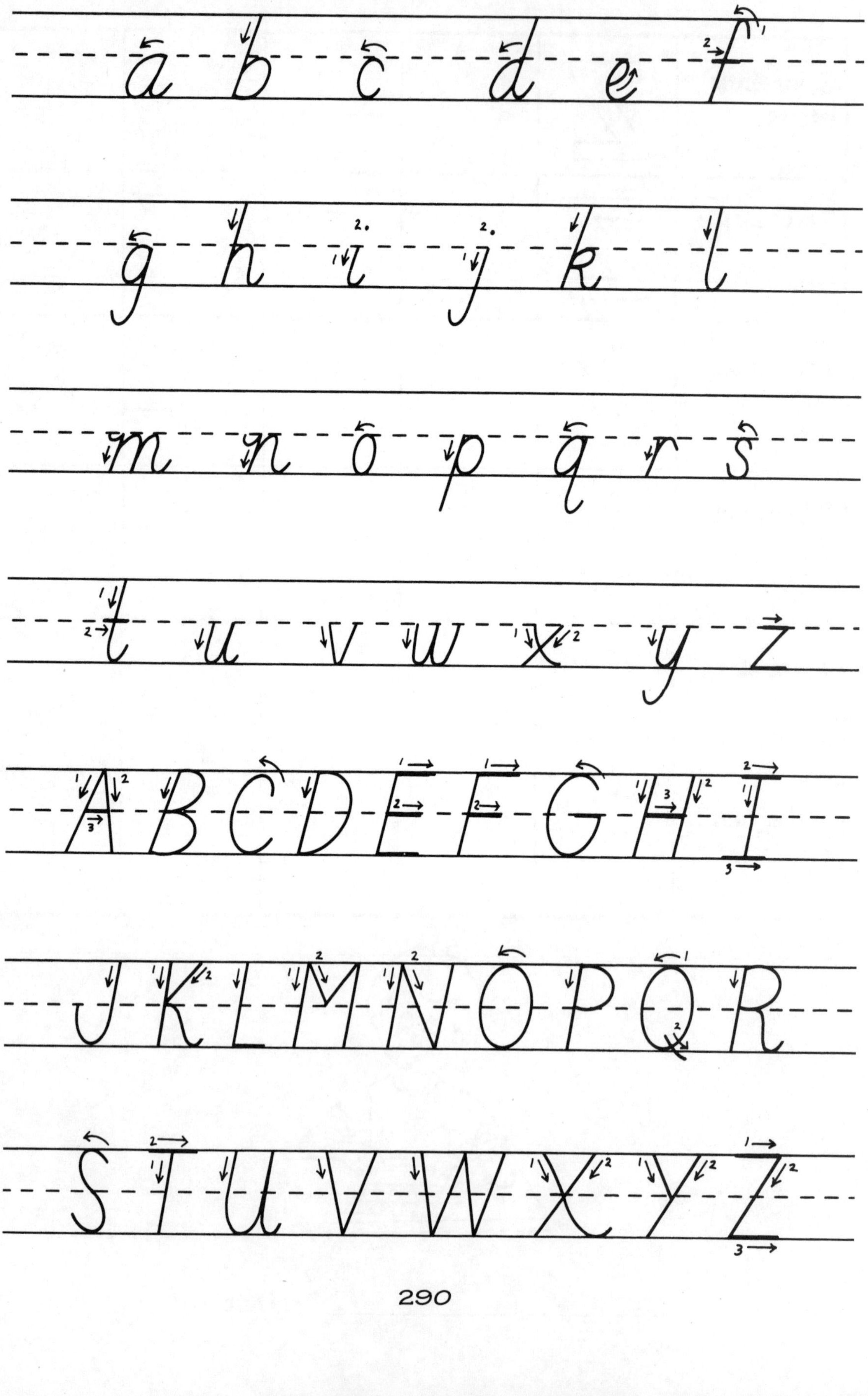

a b c d e f

g h i j k l

m n o p q r s

t u v w x y z

A B C D E F G H I

J K L M N O P Q R

S T U V W X Y Z

Lower and Upper Case Cursive Chart (NH)

a b c d e f g
h i j k l m n
o p q r s t u
v w x y z
A B C D E F G H I
J K L M N O P Q R
S T U V W X Y Z

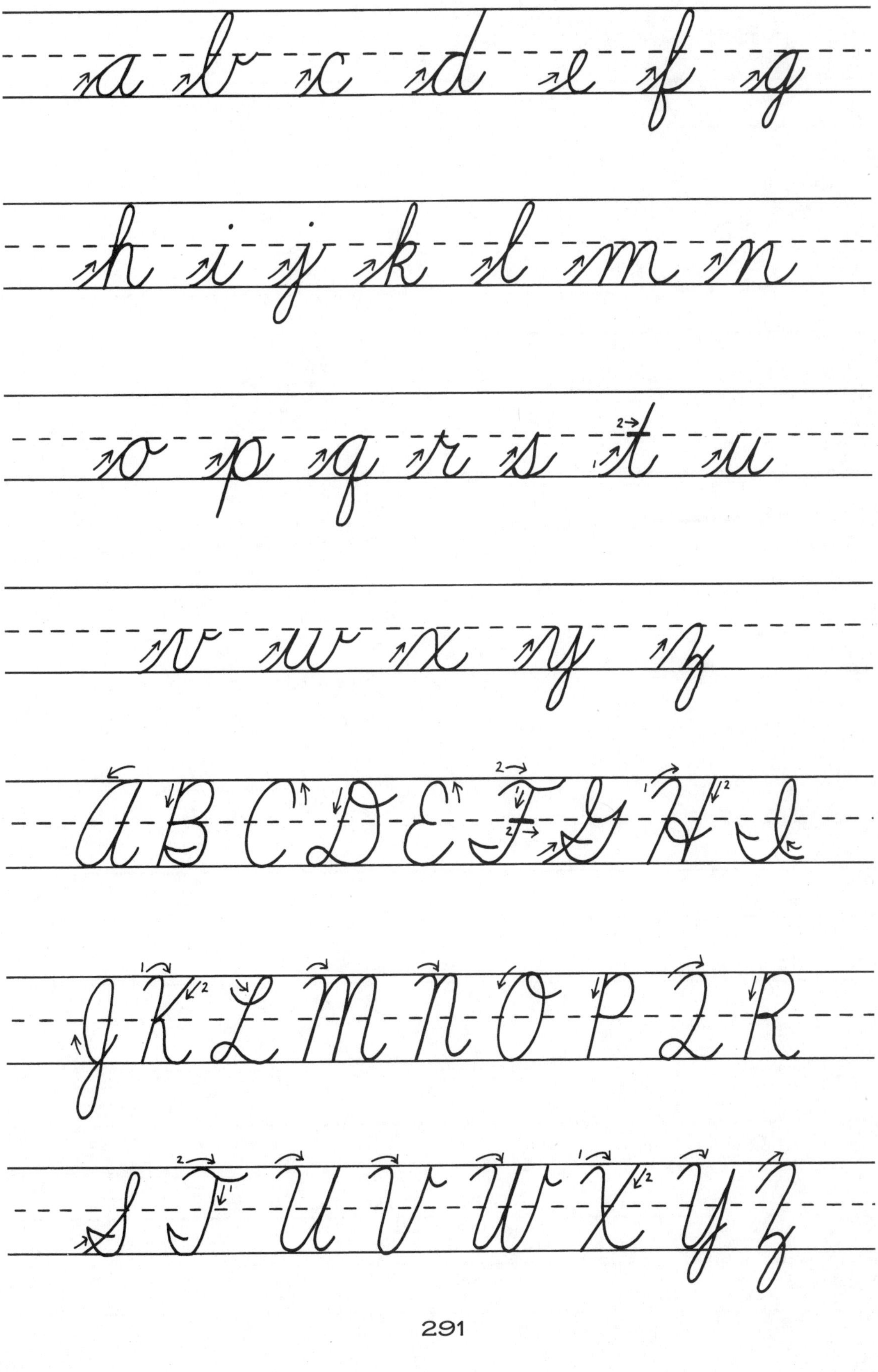

Modern Cursive Lower Case Alphabet Chart (SH)

Modern Cursive Upper Case Alphabet Chart (SH)

RESOURCES INDEX

The following resources both complement and supplement the *Ready-to-Use Fine Motor Skills & Handwriting Activities for Young Children:*

- *Ready-to-Use PE Activities Program* (K-9), Joanne M. Landy and Maxwell J. Landy (Paramus, NJ: *Prentice Hall* 1993).

- *50 Simple Ways to Raise a Child Who Is Physically Fit*, Joanne M. Landy and Keith R. Burridge (New York: *Macmillan* 1997).

- *Complete Motor Skills Activities Program*, Joanne M. Landy and Keith R. Burridge (West Nyack, NY: *The Center for Applied Research in Education* 1999).

- *Fundamental Movement Skills Computer Assessment Package*, Keith R. Burridge and Joanne M. Landy (1999), available through SPORTIME.